Visual C# 2005

A Developer's Notebook™

Jesse Liberty

O'REILLY®

Beijing · Cambridge · Farnham · Köln · Paris · Sebastopol · Taipei · Tokyo

Visual C# 2005: A Developer's Notebook™
by Jesse Liberty

Published by O'Reilly Media, Inc., 1005 Gravenstein Highway North, Sebastopol, CA 95472.

O'Reilly books may be purchased for educational, business, or sales promotional use. Online editions are also available for most titles (*safari.oreilly.com*). For more information, contact our corporate/institutional sales department: (800) 998-9938 or *corporate@oreilly.com*.

Editor:	John Osborn
Production Editor:	Sarah Sherman
Cover Designer:	Edie Freedman
Interior Designer:	David Futato

Printing History:

April 2005:	First Edition.

 This book uses RepKover,™ a durable and flexible lay-flat binding.

ISBN: 0-596-00799-X
[M]

Contents

The Developer's Notebook Series

So, you've managed to pick this book up. Cool. Really, I'm excited about that! Of course, you may be wondering why these books have the odd-looking, college notebook sort of cover. I mean, this is O'Reilly, right? Where are the animals? And, really, do you *need* another series? Couldn't this just be a cookbook? How about a nutshell, or one of those cool hacks books that seems to be everywhere? The short answer is that a developer's notebook is none of those things—in fact, it's such an important idea that we came up with an entirely new look and feel, complete with cover, fonts, and even some notes in the margin. This is all a result of trying to get something into your hands you can actually use.

It's my strong belief that while the nineties were characterized by everyone wanting to learn everything (Why not? We all had six-figure incomes from dot-com companies), the new millennium is about information pain. People don't have time (or the income) to read through 600 page books, often learning 200 things, of which only about 4 apply to their current job. It would be much nicer to just sit near one of the uber-coders and look over his shoulder, wouldn't it? To ask the guys that are neck-deep in this stuff why they chose a particular method, how they performed this one tricky task, or how they avoided that threading issue when working with piped streams. The thinking has always been that books can't serve that particular need—they can inform, and let you decide, but ultimately a coder's mind was something that couldn't really be captured on a piece of paper.

This series says that assumption is patently wrong—and we aim to prove it.

A Developer's Notebook is just what it claims to be: the often-frantic scribbling and notes that a true-blue alpha geek mentally makes when working with a new language, API, or project. It's the no-nonsense code that solves problems, stripped of page-filling commentary that often serves more as a paperweight than an epiphany. It's hackery, focused not on what is nifty or might be fun to do when you've got some free time (when's the last time that happened?), but on what you need to simply "make it work." This isn't a lecture, folks—it's a lab. If you want a lot of concept, architecture, and UML diagrams, I'll happily and proudly point you to our animal and nutshell books. If you want every answer to every problem under the sun, our omnibus cookbooks are killer. And if you are into arcane and often quirky uses of technology, hacks books simply rock. But if you're a coder, down to your core, and you just want to get on with it, then you want a Developer's Notebook. Coffee stains and all, this is from the mind of a developer to yours, barely even cleaned up enough for print. I hope you enjoy it...we sure had a good time writing them.

Notebooks Are...

Example-driven guides

As you'll see in the "Organization" section, developer's notebooks are built entirely around example code. You'll see code on nearly every page, and it's code that *does something*—not trivial "Hello World!" programs that aren't worth more than the paper they're printed on.

Aimed at developers

Ever read a book that seems to be aimed at pointy-haired bosses, filled with buzzwords, and feels more like a marketing manifesto than a programming text? We have too—and these books are the antithesis of that. In fact, a good notebook is incomprehensible to someone who can't program (don't say we didn't warn you!), and that's just the way it's supposed to be. But for developers...it's as good as it gets.

Actually enjoyable to work through

Do you really have time to sit around reading something that isn't any fun? If you do, then maybe you're into thousand-page language references—but if you're like the rest of us, notebooks are a much better fit. Practical code samples, terse dialogue centered around practical examples, and even some humor here and there—these are the ingredients of a good developer's notebook.

About doing, not talking about doing

If you want to read a book late at night without a computer nearby, these books might not be that useful. The intent is that you're coding as you go along, knee deep in bytecode. For that reason, notebooks talk code, code, code. Fire up your editor before digging in.

Notebooks Aren't...

Lectures

We don't let just anyone write a developer's notebook—you've got to be a bona fide programmer, and preferably one who stays up a little too late coding. While full-time writers, academics, and theorists are great in some areas, these books are about programming in the trenches, and are filled with instruction, not lecture.

Filled with conceptual drawings and class hierarchies

This isn't a nutshell (there, we said it). You won't find 100-page indices with every method listed, and you won't see full-page UML diagrams with methods, inheritance trees, and flow charts. What you will find is page after page of source code. Are you starting to sense a recurring theme?

Long on explanation, light on application

It seems that many programming books these days have three, four, or more chapters before you even see any working code. I'm not sure who has authors convinced that it's good to keep a reader waiting this long, but it's not anybody working on *this* series. We believe that if you're not coding within ten pages, something's wrong. These books are also chock-full of practical application, taking you from an example in a book to putting things to work on your job, as quickly as possible.

Organization

Developer's Notebooks try to communicate different information than most books, and as a result, are organized differently. They do indeed have chapters, but that's about as far as the similarity between a notebook and a traditional programming book goes. First, you'll find that all the headings in each chapter are organized around a specific task. You'll note that we said *task*, not *concept*. That's one of the important things to get about these books—they are first and foremost about doing something. Each of these headings represents a single *lab*. A lab is just what it sounds like—steps to accomplish a specific goal. In fact, that's the first heading you'll see under each lab: "How do I do that?" This is the central question of each lab, and you'll find lots of down-and-dirty code and detail in these sections. Many labs offer alternatives and address common questions about different approaches to similar problems. These are the "What about..." sections, which will help give each task some context within the programming big picture.

And one last thing—on many pages, you'll find notes scrawled in the margins of the page. These aren't for decoration; they contain tips, tricks, insights from the developers of a product, and sometimes even a little humor, just to keep you going. These notes represent part of the overall communication flow—getting you as close to reading the mind of the developer-author as we can. Hopefully they'll get you that much closer to feeling like you are indeed learning from a master.

And most of all, remember—these books are...

All Lab, No Lecture

—Brett McLaughlin, Series Creator

Preface

Who This Book Is For

Visual C# 2005: A Developer's Notebook is written for programmers who are already familiar with previous version of C# (C# 1.0 or 1.1) and who have used a previous version of Visual Studio .NET (either 2002 or 2003) to build Windows (Windows Forms) or web-based (ASP.NET) applications. My aim is to introduce you, through a series of hands-on labs, to the new features of the C# 2.0 language, the .NET 2.0 Framework, and the Visual Studio 2005 developer environment.

To get the most out of this book you'll need a copy of Visual Studio 2005 that supports C# programming. I encourage you to work your way through the labs as they are purposefully small and to the point. However, the complete source code, along with an errata sheet, a FAQ list, and links to a private support discussion center, are available on my web site, *http://www.LibertyAssociates.com* (just click Books and scroll down to Visual C# 2005: A Developer's Notebook), or at the O'Reilly web page for this book, *http://www.oreilly.com/catalog/visualcadn.*

TIP

This book went to press before the final release of Beta 2 was ready. All screenshots and code were validated against the February 2005 Community Techinal Preview. For final Beta 2 changes, please visit the O'Reilly web site for this book or visit my own web site.

Visual C# 2005: A Developer's Notebook covers very little of the material an experienced C# programmer already knows. My goal is to help you build on your current knowledge, not to waste your time demonstrating old material.

Similarly, this book does not try to be exhaustive when it comes to building Windows and web applications with the .NET 2.0 Framework or the Visual Studio 2005 developer environment. The goal is to introduce you to what is new in the language, the development environment, and the class libraries, and to equip you for further exploration of those areas that are likely to be of interest to you.

TIP

If you are not yet familiar with C# and Visual Studio, you might prefer to read *Programming C#* (O'Reilly), which teaches the entire language without assuming you are already an experienced .NET programmer.

If you are a proficient VB.NET (as opposed to VB6) programmer, on the other hand, read on; this book will teach you what you need to know to make the jump from VB.NET to C# 2.0, all in one go. (Although you'll have to work a bit harder than a C# 1.x programmer, I believe you'll find that most of the syntactic differences between VB and C# are trivial and obvious.) For more information, see the *C# AND VB.NET Conversion Pocket Reference* (O'Reilly).

How This Book Is Organized

The goal of *Visual C# 2005: A Developer's Notebook* is to equip you to create meaningful applications; not just to learn about changes to the C# language. The book is organized into five chapters. Each chapter consists of a series of labs, each of which introduces a new feature, shows how it's used, and then walks you through an example, explaining the details you need to understand along the way. Each lab includes a "What about..." section that attempts to anticipate and answer follow-up questions, as well as (perhaps most importantly) a section that tells you where you can learn more about each topic.

Chapter 1 explains what is new in the language. We start by examining one of the most anticipated features of C# 2.0, generics, and we explore them in-depth. The chapter also includes coverage of the new iterators, anonymous methods, and partial types that are part of C# 2.0, as well as static classes, nullable types, accessing objects in the Global namespace, and limiting access to fields within properties. The chapter closes with a brief discussion of delegate covariance and contravariance.

Chapter 2 explores the changes and improvements made to Visual Studio 2005. You will see how to configure the new development platform and how to put the enhanced editor to work for you. A very exciting new feature within Visual Studio 2005 is automated refactoring. The software also now offers better support for code re-use through predefined code snippets. Debugging is discussed and the new visualizers are demonstrated.

Because I assume you're learning C# 2.0 to create applications, the rest of the book focuses on just that. Chapter 3 demonstrates the new features available to you for creating Windows applications, including the new ToolStrips, masking, auto-complete text boxes, split windows, and support for adding Windows system sounds. The new data controls for Windows Forms are demonstrated, as is ClickOnce deployment, a new feature that greatly improves the feasibility of using rich clients or so-called Smart Clients, for certain kinds of networked applications.

Chapter 4 is all about new features for building web applications, some of which are found in the ASP.NET 2.0 Framework libraries and others in the Visual Studio 2005 IDE. The goal of the ASP.NET 2.0 development team was to make it possible to build web applications with 75% less code than was required for ASP.NET 1.x applications. Their success is remarkable. Chapter 4 covers the new controls that facilitate security, authentication, and personalization, as well as new support for creating uniform and coherent sites with themes and master pages.

Finally, Chapter 5 focuses on the new .NET 2.0 controls for data access along with revisions to the ADO.NET classes. Topics include creating master/detail records with no code and integrating XML data sources into your application.

Where Can I Learn More?

The goal of this book is to introduce you to new features of C# 2.0, .NET 2.0, and the Visual Studio 2005 developer environment that are likely to be of greatest interest to C# programmers. The Developer's Notebook series is not an exhaustive reference. Thus, at the end of each lab you'll find a section titled "Where can I learn more?" Here I will point you to books, magazine articles, online resources, Microsoft Developer Network (MSDN) articles, and Visual Studio 2005 Help entries and tell you where you can find more detail or obtain another perspective. When I refer to the *MSDN Library*, I am generally referring to the MSDN Library that is available to you through the installed Visual Studio 2005 Help, or online at *http://msdn.microsoft.com/library*. MSDN subscribers also receive the library on DVD from time to time as part of their regular monthly updates. I also point to articles and resources found elsewhere at the official MSDN site, or at related sites such as Channel 9 (*http://channel9.msdn.com/default.aspx*) and GotDotNet (*http://www.gotdotnet.com*).

What You Need to Use This Book

The most important requirement for this book is a solid familiarity with C# 1.x and experience building .NET applications. I do not hold your hand through the fundamentals; instead, I focus on what is new in the 2005 edition.

You'll want a computer with a version of Visual Studio 2005 installed that supports C# 2.0, along with one or another form of SQL Server (SQL Server Express is fine).

You can also do the labs in this book using the new Visual Studio Express Editions. You'll need both Visual C# 2005 Express Edition (for Chapters 1, 2, 3, and 5) and Visual Web Developer 2005 Express Edition (for Chapter 4).

Conventions Used in This Book

The following typographical conventions are used in this book:

Plain text
> Indicates menu titles, menu options, menu buttons, and keyboard accelerators (such as Alt and Ctrl).

Italic
> Indicates new terms, URLs, email addresses, filenames, file extensions, pathnames, directories, and Unix utilities.

Constant width
> Indicates commands, options, switches, variables, attributes, keys, functions, types, classes, namespaces, methods, modules, properties, parameters, values, objects, events, event handlers, XML tags, HTML tags, macros, the contents of files, and the output from commands.

Constant width bold
> Shows commands and other text that should be typed literally by the user.

Constant width italic
> Shows text that should be replaced with user-supplied values.

TIP

This icon signifies a tip, suggestion, or general note.

WARNING

This icon indicates a warning or caution.

Using Code Examples

This book is to help you get your job done. In general, you may use the code in this book in your programs and documentation. You do not need to contact us for permission unless you're reproducing a significant portion of the code. For example, writing a program that uses several chunks of code from this book does not require permission. Selling or distributing a CD-ROM of examples from O'Reilly books *does* require permission. Answering a question by citing this book and quoting example code does not require permission. Incorporating a significant amount of example code from this book into your product's documentation *does* require permission.

We appreciate, but do not require, attribution. An attribution usually includes the title, author, publisher, and ISBN. For example: "*Visual C# 2005: A Developer's Notebook*, First Edition, by Jesse Liberty. Copyright 2005 O'Reilly Media, Inc., 0-596-00799-X."

If you feel your use of code examples falls outside fair use or the permission given here, feel free to contact us at *permissions@oreilly.com*.

I'd Like to Hear from You

Please send all your comments, suggestions, and (horrors!) errata to *jliberty@libertyassociates.com*. Please check the FAQ list and errata sheet on my web site (*http://www.LibertyAssociates.com*; click Books) first, though, as someone might have already reported your error or asked your question.

You can get extensive help through the private discussion group provided for this book. Sign up through my web site. Then follow the link to the discussion forum provided at the top of the Books page.

Comments and Questions

Please address comments and questions concerning this book to the publisher:

O'Reilly Media, Inc.
1005 Gravenstein Highway North
Sebastopol, CA 95472
(800) 998-9938 (in the United States or Canada)
(707) 829-0515 (international or local)
(707) 829-0104 (fax)

We have a web page for this book, where we list errata, examples, and any additional information. You can access this page at:

http://www.oreilly.com/catalog/visualcadn

To comment or ask technical questions about this book, send email to:

bookquestions@oreilly.com

For more information about our books, conferences, Resource Centers, and the O'Reilly Network, see our web site at:

http://www.oreilly.com

Safari Enabled

 When you see a Safari® enabled icon on the cover of your favorite technology book that means the book is available online through the O'Reilly Network Safari Bookshelf.

Safari offers a solution that's better than e-books. It's a virtual library that lets you easily search thousands of top tech books, cut and paste code samples, download chapters, and find quick answers when you need the most accurate, current information. Try it for free at *http://safari.oreilly.com*.

Acknowledgments

The author is deeply grateful to O'Reilly Media for inventing this incredible series, and to John Osborn both for bringing me into O'Reilly and for letting me write this book.

This book has had some of the best technical editors I've ever had the pleasure to work with, including Nicholas Paldino, Luke Hoban, Michael Weinhardt, and Bill Hamilton.

In addition, a number of faithful readers agreed to provide feedback while the book was being written, including Cristof Falk, Frank Gilgic, Christopher Kimpbell, Daniel O'Connel, Jon Skeet, Dan Nash, Zheng Tianbo, Colin Young, Girish Bharadwaj, Brian Bischof, David Bench, Mattias Sjogren, Jouko Kynsijarvi, Rob Bazinet, Rakesh Rajan, Willem van Rumpt, Joseph Sign, Michael Rodriguez, Jon George, Ross Gray, Vance Kessler, James Thomas, David Novak, and especially Sahil Malik, Carel Blumenstock, Rolf M. Marsh, Michael Taylor, and Jamie McQuay. Their help was invaluable.

Dedication

This book is dedicated to the 70 million victims of AIDS who became ill due to the initial indifference of others. Writing good code is a great calling, as long as we look up from the computer once in a while.

C# 2.0

In this chapter, you will learn about and use the new features in C# 2.0, including generics, iterators, anonymous methods, partial types, static classes, nullable types, and limiting access to properties, as well as delegate covariance and contravariance.

Probably the most exciting and most anticipated new feature in C# 2.0 is generics, which provide you with quick and easy type-safe collections. So, let's start there.

Create a Type-Safe List Using a Generic Collection

Type safety is the key to creating code that's easy to maintain. A type-safe language (and framework) finds bugs at compile time (reliably) rather than at runtime (usually after you've shipped the product!). The key weakness in C# 1.x was the absence of *generics*, which enable you to declare a general collection (for example, a stack or a list) that can accept members of any type yet will be type-safe at compile time.

In Version 1.x of the framework, nearly all the collections were declared to hold instances of System.Object, and because *everything* derives from System.Object, these collections could hold any type at all; that is, they were not type-safe.

Suppose, for example, you were creating a list of Employee objects in C# 1.x. To do so, you would use an ArrayList, which holds objects of the System.Object type. Adding new Employees to the collection was not a problem because Employees were derived from System.Object, but when you tried to retrieve an Employee from the ArrayList, all you would get back was an Object reference, which you would then have to cast:

```
Employee theEmployee = (Employee) myArrayList[1];
```

An even bigger problem, however, was that there was nothing to stop you from adding a string or some other type to the ArrayList. As long as you never needed to access the string, you would never note the errant type. Suppose, however, that you passed that ArrayList to a method that expected an ArrayList of Employee objects. When that method attempted to cast the String object to the Employee type at runtime, an exception would be thrown.

A final problem with .NET 1.x collections arose when you added value types to the collection. Value types had to be boxed on their way into the collection and explicitly unboxed on their way out.

.NET 2.0 eliminates all these problems with a new library of collections, which you will find in the System.Collections.Generic namespace. A *generic collection* is simply a collection that allows you to specify its member types when you declare it. Once declared, the compiler will allow only objects of that type to be added to your list. You define generic collections using special syntax; the syntax uses angle brackets to indicate variables that must be defined when an instance of the collection is declared.

With generic collections your code is type-safe, easier to maintain, and simpler to use.

There is no need to cast when you retrieve objects from a generic collection, and your code is safer, easier to maintain, and simpler to use than it is with untyped collections such as ArrayList.

How do I do that?

To get a feel for the new generic types in .NET 2.0, let's use the type-safe List class to create a list of employees. To execute this lab, open Visual Studio 2005, create a new C# Console application, and name it CreateATypeSafeList. Replace the code Visual Studio 2005 creates for you with the code in Example 1-1.

TIP

You must use the System.Collections.Generic namespace to use the generic types. By default Visual Studio 2005 adds this namespace to all projects.

Example 1-1. Creating a type-safe list

```
using System;
using System.Collections.Generic;

namespace CreateATypeSafeList
{
```

Example 1-1. Creating a type-safe list (continued)

```csharp
// a class to store in the List
public class Employee
{
    private int empID;

    // constructor
    public Employee(int empID)
    {
        this.empID = empID;
    }

    // override the ToString method to
    // display this employee's id
    public override string ToString()
    {
        return empID.ToString();
    }
}        // end class

// Test driver class
public class Program
{
    // entry point
    static void Main()
    {
        // Declare the type safe list (of Employee objects)
        List<Employee> empList = new List<Employee>();

        // Declare a second type safe list (of integers)
        List<int> intList = new List<int>();

        // populate the Lists
        for (int i = 0; i < 5; i++)
        {
            empList.Add(new Employee(i + 100));
            intList.Add(i * 5);
            // empList.Add(i * 5);   // see "What About" section below
        }

        // print the integer list
        foreach (int i in intList)
        {
            Console.Write("{0} ", i.ToString());
        }

        Console.WriteLine("\n");

        // print the Employee List
        foreach (Employee employee in empList)
        {
            Console.Write("{0} ", employee.ToString());
        }
```

Example 1-1. Creating a type-safe list (continued)

```
        Console.WriteLine("\n");
      }
   }
}
```

Output:

```
0 5 10 15 20
100 101 102 103 104
```

TIP

All the source code for the labs in this chapter is available on my web site, *http://www.LibertyAssociates.com*. Click Books, and then scroll down to C# 2.0 Programmer's Notebook and click Source to save the source code to your computer.

Once unzipped, the source code is in chapter folders, and each lab folder is named with the namespace shown in the listing. For instance, for Example 1-1, the source is stored in *Chapter 1\ CreateATypeSafeList*.

While you are at my site, you can also read the FAQ list and errata sheet and join a private support discussion forum.

What just happened?

This listing creates two classes: an Employee class to be held in the collection and the Program class created by Visual Studio 2005. It also uses the List class provided by the .NET Framework Class Library.

The Employee class contains a single private field (empID), a constructor, and an override of ToString to return the empID field as a string.

First you create an instance of List that will hold Employee objects. The type of empList is "List of Employee Objects" and is declared thus:

```
List<Employee> empList
```

When you see the definition List<T>, the T is a placeholder for the actual type you'll place in that list.

As always, empList is just a reference to the object you create on the heap using the new keyword. The new keyword expects you to invoke a constructor, which you do as follows:

```
new List<Employee>( )
```

This creates an instance of "List of Employee Objects" on the heap, and the entire statement, put together, assigns a reference to that new object to empList:

```
List<Employee> empList = new List<Employee>();
```

TIP

This is just like writing:

```
Dog milo = new Dog();
```

in which you create an instance of Dog on the heap and assign it to the reference to Dog, milo.

In the next statement, you create a second List, this time of type "List of Integers":

```
List<int> intList = new List<int>();
```

Now you are free to add integers to the list of integers, and Employee objects to the list of Employee objects. Once the lists are populated, you can iterate through each of them, using a foreach loop to display their contents in the console window:

```
foreach (Employee employee in empList)
{
    Console.Write("{0} ", employee.ToString());
}
```

What about...

...if you try to add an integer to the list of Employees?

Try it. Start by uncommenting the following line in Example 1-1 and recompiling the program:

```
empList.Add(i * 5);
```

You'll get a pair of compile errors:

```
Error   1     The best overloaded method match for 'System.Collections.
Generic.List<ListCollection.Employee>.Add(ListCollection.Employee)' has some
invalid arguments
Error   2     Argument '1': cannot convert from 'int' to
'ListCollection.Employee'
```

The information provided in these two compile errors enable you to determine that it is not legal to add an int to a collection of Employee objects because no implicit conversion or subtype relationship exists from one to the other.

The good news is that this is a compile error, rather than a runtime error, which can sneak out the door and happen only when your client runs the application!

…what about other generic collections; are any available?

Other generic collections are available as well. For instance, the Stack and Queue collections, as well as the ICollection interface, are available in type-safe versions in .NET 2.0.

You use these just as you would List<T>. For example, to make a stack of Employee objects, you replace T in the Stack definition (Stack<T>) with the Employee type:

```
Stack<Employee> employeeStack = new Stack<Employee>();
```

You can store derived types in a type-safe collection. Thus, a collection of Employees will hold a Manager object, if Manager derives from Employee.

Where can I learn more?

You can learn about all the .NET 2.0 generic classes in the MSDN topic titled "Commonly Used Collection Types," and you can read an article on the subject on O'Reilly's ONDotnet.com site at *http://www.ondotnet.com/pub/a/dotnet/2004/05/17/liberty.html*.

TIP

A document on my web site lists the links I mention in each lab so that you can copy and paste them into your browser. To get it, go to *http://www.LibertyAssociates.com*, click Books, scroll down to *Visual C# 2005: A Developer's Notebook*, and click Links.doc.

The next lab will show you how to create your own type-safe collections to supplement those provided by the Framework.

Create Your Own Generic Collection

.NET 2.0 provides a number of generic collection classes for lists, stacks, queues, dictionaries, etc. Typically, these are more than sufficient for your programming needs. But from time to time you might decide to create your own generic collection classes, such as when you want to provide those collections with problem-specific knowledge or capabilities that are simply not available in existing collections (for example, creating an optimized linked list, or adding generic collection semantics to another class you've created). It is a goal of the language and the Framework to empower you to create your own generic collection types.

From time to time you will decide to create your own generic collection classes.

How do I do that?

The easiest way to create a generic collection class is to create a specific collection (for example, one that holds integers) and then replace the type (for example, int) with the generic type (for example, T).

Thus:

```
private int data;
```

becomes:

```
private T data;   // T is a generic Type Parameter
```

The generic type parameter (in this case, T) is defined by you when you create your collection class by placing the type parameter inside angle brackets (< >):

```
public class Node<T>
```

TIP

Many programmers use T for "type," but Microsoft recommends you use longer, more descriptive type names (for example, Node<DocumentType>).

Now you have defined a new type, "Node of T," which at runtime will become "Node of int" or node of any other type the compiler recognizes.

Example 1-2 creates a linked list of nodes of T, and then uses two instances of that generic list, each holding a different type of object.

Example 1-2. Creating your own generic collection

```
using System;

namespace GenericLinkedList
{
    public class Pilgrim
    {
        private string name;
        public Pilgrim(string name)
        {
            this.name = name;
        }
        public override string ToString( )
        {
            return this.name;
        }
    }
    public class Node<T>
    {
        // member fields
```

Example 1-2. Creating your own generic collection (continued)

```
private T data;
private Node<T> next = null;

// constructor
public Node(T data)
{
   this.data = data;
}

// properties
public T Data { get { return this.data; } }

public Node<T> Next
{
   get { return this.next; }
}

// methods
public void Append(Node<T> newNode)
{
   if (this.next == null)
   {
      this.next = newNode;
   }
   else
   {
      next.Append(newNode);
   }
}
public override string ToString()
{
   string output = data.ToString();

   if (next != null)
   {
      output += ", " + next.ToString();
   }

   return output;
}
}     // end class


public class LinkedList<T>
{
   // member fields
   private Node<T> headNode = null;

   // properties

   // indexer
   public T this[int index]
```

Example 1-2. Creating your own generic collection (continued)

```
{
    get
    {
        int ctr = 0;
        Node<T> node = headNode;

        while (node != null && ctr <= index)
        {
            if (ctr == index)
            {
                return node.Data;
            }
            else
            {
                node = node.Next;
            }

            ++ctr;
        } // end while
        throw new ArgumentOutOfRangeException( );
    }       // end get
}              // end indexer


// constructor
public LinkedList( )
{
}

// methods
public void Add(T data)
{
    if (headNode == null)
    {
        headNode = new Node<T>(data);
    }
    else
    {
        headNode.Append(new Node<T>(data));
    }
}
public override string ToString( )
{
    if (this.headNode != null)
    {
        return this.headNode.ToString( );
    }
    else
    {
        return string.Empty;
    }
}
```

Example 1-2. Creating your own generic collection (continued)

```
    }

    class Program
    {
        static void Main(string[ ] args)
        {
            LinkedList<int> myLinkedList = new LinkedList<int>();
            for (int i = 0; i < 10; i++)
            {
                myLinkedList.Add(i);
            }

            Console.WriteLine("Integers: " + myLinkedList);
            LinkedList<Pilgrim> pilgrims = new LinkedList<Pilgrim>();
            pilgrims.Add(new Pilgrim("The Knight"));
            pilgrims.Add(new Pilgrim("The Miller"));
            pilgrims.Add(new Pilgrim("The Reeve"));
            pilgrims.Add(new Pilgrim("The Cook"));

            Console.WriteLine("Pilgrims: " + pilgrims);
            Console.WriteLine("The fourth integer is " + myLinkedList[3]);
            Pilgrim d = pilgrims[1];
            Console.WriteLine("The second pilgrim is " + d);
        }
    }
}
```

Output:

```
Integers: 0, 1, 2, 3, 4, 5, 6, 7, 8, 9
Pilgrims: The Knight, The Miller, The Reeve, The Cook
The fourth integer is 3
The second pilgrim is The Miller
```

What just happened?

You just created a *generic* linked list; one that is type-safe for any type of object you hold in the collection. In fact, one way to create a linked list such as this is to start by creating a type-specific linked list. This simple example works by defining a generic linked list whose head node is initialized to null:

```
public class LinkedList<T>
{
    private Node<T> headNode = null;
    ...
}
```

When you add data to the linked list, a new node is created and if there is no head node, that new node becomes the head; otherwise, append is called on the head node.

Each node checks to see if its next field is null (and thus the current node is the end of the list). If so, the current node appends the new node; otherwise, it passes the new node to the next member in the list.

Notice that LinkedList is intentionally declared with the same generic type parameter as Node. Because they both use the same letter (T), the compiler knows that the type used to substitute for T in LinkedList will be the same type used to substitute for T in Node. This makes sense: a linked list of integers will hold nodes of integers.

Creating collections with generics is far easier than you might imagine. The simplest way to approach the problem is to build a type-specific collection, and then replace the type with the generic <T>.

What about...

...using generics with other code structures? Can I do that?

Sure; you also can use generics with structs, interfaces, delegates, and even methods.

Where can I learn more?

For more about creating your own class with generics, see the MSDN Help file, "Topic: Generics," as well as the article mentioned previously on O'Reilly's ONDotnet.com site at *http://www.ondotnet.com/pub/a/ dotnet/2004/05/17/liberty.html*. Also, an open "Community Project to Develop the Best Public License Collection Classes for .NET" is available on the Wintellect site at *http://www.wintellect.com/powercollections/*.

Implement the Collection Interfaces

In addition to its generic collection classes, .NET 2.0 also provides a set of generic interfaces that enable you to create type-safe collections that have all the functionality of the earlier, nongeneric .NET 1.x collection types. You'll find these interfaces in the System.Collections.Generic namespace. The namespace also includes a number of related generic interfaces, such as IComparable<T>, which you can use to compare two objects of type T regardless of whether they are part of a collection.

You can create a sorted linked list by having each datatype stored in the list implement the IComparable<T> interface and by having your Node object be responsible for inserting each new Node at the correct (sorted) position in the linked list.

How do I do that?

Integer already implements IComparable; you can easily modify Pilgrim to do so as well. Modify the definition of the Pilgrim class to indicate that it implements the IComparable<T> interface:

```
public class Pilgrim : IComparable<Pilgrim>
```

Be sure to implement the CompareTo and the Equals methods that the interface requires. The objects these methods receive will be of type Pilgrim because this is a type-safe interface, not a "standard" interface that would pass in objects:

```
public int CompareTo(Pilgrim rhs)
public bool Equals(Pilgrim rhs)
```

You can constrain the datatypes your generic type accepts by using constraints.

All you need to do now is change the logic of adding a node. This time, instead of adding to the end of the list, you'll insert the new node into the list where it belongs based on the implementation of the CompareTo method.

For this to work, you must ensure that the datatype held in the node implements IComparable. You accomplish this with a constraint using the keyword where:

```
public class Node<T> : IComparable<Node<T>> where T:IComparable<T>
```

This line of code declares a class Node of T that implements IComparable (of Node of T) and that is constrained to hold datatypes that implement IComparable. If you try to have your Node class hold an object that does not implement IComparable, you will receive an error message when you attempt to compile it.

You must be careful to return the new head of the list if the new node is "less than" the current head of the list, as shown in Example 1-3 (Changes from the previous example are highlighted.)

Example 1-3. Implementing generic interfaces

```
using System;
using System.Collections.Generic;

namespace ImplementingGenericInterfaces
{
    public class Pilgrim : IComparable<Pilgrim>
    {
        private string name;
        public Pilgrim(string name)
        {
            this.name = name;
        }
        public override string ToString()
```

Example 1-3. Implementing generic interfaces (continued)

```
    {
        return this.name;
    }

    // implement the interface
    public int CompareTo(Pilgrim rhs)
    {
        return this.name.CompareTo(rhs.name);
    }
    public bool Equals(Pilgrim rhs)
    {
        return this.name == rhs.name;
    }
}


// node must implement IComparable of Node of T
// constrain Nodes to only take items that implement Icomparable
// by using the where keyword.
public class Node<T> : IComparable<Node<T>> where T:IComparable<T>
{
    // member fields
    private T data;
    private Node<T> next = null;
    private Node<T> prev = null;

    // constructor
    public Node(T data)
    {
        this.data = data;
    }

    // properties
    public T Data { get { return this.data; } }

    public Node<T> Next
    {
        get { return this.next; }
    }

    public int CompareTo(Node<T> rhs)
    {
        // this works because of the constraint
        return data.CompareTo(rhs.data);
    }

    public bool Equals(Node<T> rhs)
    {
        return this.data.Equals(rhs.data);
    }
```

Example 1-3. *Implementing generic interfaces (continued)*

```
// methods
public Node<T> Add(Node<T> newNode)
{
    if (this.CompareTo(newNode) > 0) // goes before me
    {
        newNode.next = this;   // new node points to me

        // if I have a previous, set it to point to
        // the new node as its next
        if (this.prev != null)
        {
            this.prev.next = newNode;
            newNode.prev = this.prev;
        }
        // set prev in current node to point to new node
        this.prev = newNode;
        // return the newNode in case it is the new head
        return newNode;
    }
    else          // goes after me
    {
        // if I have a next, pass the new node along for comparison
        if (this.next != null)
        {
            this.next.Add(newNode);
        }
        // I don't have a next so set the new node
            // to be my next and set its prev to point to me.
        else
        {
            this.next = newNode;
            newNode.prev = this;
        }
        return this;
    }
}

public override string ToString()
{
    string output = data.ToString();

    if (next != null)
    {
        output += ", " + next.ToString();
    }

    return output;
}
}     // end class
```

Example 1-3. Implementing generic interfaces (continued)

```
public class SortedLinkedList<T> where T : IComparable<T>
{
    // member fields
    private Node<T>  headNode = null;


    // properties

    // indexer
    public T this[int index]
    {
        get
        {
            int ctr = 0;
            Node<T> node = headNode;

            while (node != null && ctr <= index)
            {
                if (ctr == index)
                {
                    return node.Data;
                }
                else
                {
                    node = node.Next;
                }

                ++ctr;
            } // end while
            throw new ArgumentOutOfRangeException( );
        }     // end get
    }          // end indexer


    // constructor
    public SortedLinkedList( )
    {
    }

    // methods
    public void Add(T data)
    {
        if (headNode == null)
        {
            headNode = new Node<T>(data);
        }
        else
        {
            headNode = headNode.Add(new Node<T>(data));
        }
    }
```

Example 1-3. *Implementing generic interfaces (continued)*

```csharp
    public override string ToString()
    {
        if (this.headNode != null)
        {
            return this.headNode.ToString();
        }
        else
        {
            return string.Empty;
        }
    }
}

class Program
{
    // entry point
    static void Main(string[] args)
    {
        SortedLinkedList<int> mySortedLinkedList = new SortedLinkedList<int>();
        Random rand = new Random();
        Console.Write("Adding: ");
        for (int i = 0; i < 10; i++)
        {
            int nextInt = rand.Next(10);
            Console.Write("{0}  ", nextInt);
            mySortedLinkedList.Add(nextInt);
        }

        SortedLinkedList<Pilgrim> pilgrims = new SortedLinkedList<Pilgrim>();
        pilgrims.Add(new Pilgrim("The Knight"));
        pilgrims.Add(new Pilgrim("The Miller"));
        pilgrims.Add(new Pilgrim("The Reeve"));
        pilgrims.Add(new Pilgrim("The Cook"));
        pilgrims.Add(new Pilgrim("The Man of Law"));

        Console.WriteLine("\nRetrieving collections...");

        DisplayList<int>("Integers", mySortedLinkedList);
        DisplayList<Pilgrim>("Pilgrims", pilgrims);
        //Console.WriteLine("Integers: " + mySortedLinkedList);
        //Console.WriteLine("Pilgrims: " + pilgrims);

        Console.WriteLine("The fourth integer is " + mySortedLinkedList[3]);
        Pilgrim d = pilgrims[2];
        Console.WriteLine("The third pilgrim is " + d);
//          foreach (Pilgrim p in pilgrims)
//          {
//              Console.WriteLine("The pilgrim's name is " + p.ToString());
//          }
    } // end main
```

Example 1-3. Implementing generic interfaces (continued)

```
    private static void DisplayList<T>(string intro, SortedLinkedList<T>
theList)
        where T : IComparable<T>
    {
        Console.WriteLine(intro + ": " + theList);
    }
}   // end class
}       // end namespace
```

Output:

```
Adding: 2  8  2  5  1  7  2  8  5  5
Retrieving collections...
Integers: 1, 2, 2, 5, 7, 8, 8
Pilgrims: The Cook, The Knight, The Man of Law, The Miller, The Reeve
The fourth integer is 5
The third pilgrim is The Man of Law
```

What just happened?

The Pilgrim class changed just enough to implement the generic IComparable interface. The linked list didn't change at all, but the Node class did undergo some changes to support the sorted list.

First, the Node class was marked to implement IComparable and was constrained to hold only objects that themselves implement IComparable:

```
public class Node<T> : IComparable<Node<T>> where T:IComparable<T>
```

Second, Node added a reference to the previous node, in addition to the next node (making this a doubly linked list):

```
private Node<T> next = null;
private Node<T> prev = null;
```

The Node class must implement CompareTo and Equals. These are simple to implement because the constraint ensures that the data you are comparing also implements IComparable:

```
public int CompareTo(Node<T> rhs)
{
    // this works because of the constraint
    data.CompareTo(rhs.data);
}
```

What about...

...the IComparable requirement? Why did Pilgrim and Node require IComparable, but the linked list did not?

To understand this, it's important to note that both Pilgrims and Nodes must be compared; linked lists are not compared. Because the linked list is sorted by sorting its nodes, there is no need to compare two linked lists to see which one is "greater" than the other.

...what about passing generic types to a method; can I do that?

Yes, you can pass a generic type to a method, but only if the method is generic. In Example 1-3, you display the contents of the list of integers and the list of pilgrims with the following code:

```
Console.WriteLine("Integers: " + myLinkedList);
Console.WriteLine("Pilgrims: " + pilgrims);
```

You are free to create a method to take these lists and display them (or manipulate them):

```
private void DisplayList<T>(string intro, LinkedList<T> theList) where T :
IComparable<T>
{
    Console.WriteLine(intro + ": " + theList);
}
```

When you call the method, you supply the type:

```
DisplayList<int>("Integers", myLinkedList);
DisplayList<Pilgrim>("Pilgrims", pilgrims);
```

TIP

The compiler is capable of type inference, so you can rewrite the preceding two lines as follows:

```
DisplayList("Integers", myLinkedList);
DisplayList("Pilgrims", pilgrims);
```

Where can I learn more?

The MSDN Library covers the Generic namespace extensively. Search on Systems.Collections.Generic. Also, see my article on generics on O'Reilly's ONDotnet.com site at *http://www.ondotnet.com/pub/a/dotnet/2004/05/17/liberty.html*.

Enumerate Using Generic Iterators

In the previous examples you could not iterate over your list of Pilgrims using a foreach loop. As such, if you try to use the following code in Example 1-3:

```
foreach ( Pilgrim p in pilgrims )
{
    Console.WriteLine("The pilgrim's name is " + p.ToString());
}
```

you will receive the following error:

```
Error      1      foreach statement cannot operate on variables of type
'ImplementingGenericInterfaces.LinkedList <ImplementingGenericInterfaces.
Pilgrim>' because 'ImplementingGenericInterfaces.LinkedList
<ImplementingGenericInterfaces.Pilgrim>' does not contain a public
definition for 'GetEnumerator'
```

Adding iterators allows a client to iterate over your class using foreach.

In earlier versions of C#, implementing GetEnumerator was somewhat complicated and always tedious, but in C# 2.0 it is greatly simplified.

How do I do that?

To simplify the process of creating iterators, we'll begin by simplifying both the Pilgrim class and the Linked List class. The Linked List class will forgo all use of nodes and will store its contents in a fixed-size array (as the simplest type-safe container imaginable). Thus, it is a Linked List in name only! This will allow us to focus on the implementation of the IEnumerator interface, as shown in Example 1-4.

Example 1-4. Implementing IEnumerator, simplified

```
#region Using directives

using System;
using System.Collections.Generic;
using System.Text;

#endregion

namespace SimplifiedEnumerator
{
    // simplified Pilgrim
    public class Pilgrim
    {
        private string name;
        public Pilgrim(string name)
        {
            this.name = name;
```

Example 1-4. Implementing IEnumerator, simplified (continued)

```csharp
        }
        public override string ToString()
        {
            return this.name;
        }

    }

    // simplified Linked List
    class NotReallyALinkedList<T> : IEnumerable<T>
    {
        // the entire linked list is stored in this
        // fixed size array
        T[] myArray;

        // constructor takes an array and stores the members
        public NotReallyALinkedList(T[] members)
        {
            myArray = members;
        }

        // implement the method for IEnumerable
        IEnumerator<T> IEnumerable<T>.GetEnumerator()
        {
            foreach (T t in this.myArray)
            {
                yield return t;
            }
        }
System.Collections.IEnumerator System.Collections.IEnumerable.GetEnumerator()
{
    throw new NotImplementedException();
}
    }


    class Program
    {
        static void Main(string[] args)
        {
            // hardcode a string array of Pilgrim objects
            Pilgrim[] pilgrims = new Pilgrim[5];
            pilgrims[0] = new Pilgrim("The Knight");
            pilgrims[1] = new Pilgrim("The Miller");
            pilgrims[2] = new Pilgrim("The Reeve");
            pilgrims[3] = new Pilgrim("The Cook");
            pilgrims[4] = new Pilgrim("The Man Of Law");

            // create the linked list, pass in the array
            NotReallyALinkedList<Pilgrim> pilgrimCollection =
                new NotReallyALinkedList<Pilgrim>(pilgrims);
```

Example 1-4. Implementing IEnumerator, simplified (continued)

```
        // iterate through the linked list
        foreach (Pilgrim p in pilgrimCollection)
        {
            Console.WriteLine(p);
        }
    }
  }
}
```

Output:

```
The Knight
The Miller
The Reeve
The Cook
The Man Of Law
```

What just happened?

In this example, the linked list is greatly simplified to keep its members in an array (in fact, it is not really a linked list at all). Because you've made your pseudo-LinkedList enumerable, however, now you can enumerate the Pilgrims in the pilgrims collection using a foreach loop.

When you write:

```
foreach (Pilgrim p in pilgrimCollection)
```

the C# compiler invokes the GetEnumerator method of the class. Internally, it looks more or less like this:

```
Enumerator e = pilgrimCollection.GetEnumerator();
while (e.MoveNext())
{
    Pilgrim p = e.Current;
}
```

Whenever you call foreach, the compiler internally translates it to a call to GetEnumerator.

As noted earlier, in C# 2.0 you do not have to worry about implementing MoveNext() or the current property. You need only use the new C# keyword yield.

TIP

You use yield only in iterator blocks. It either provides a value to the enumerator object or it signals the end of the iteration:

```
yield return expression;
yield break;
```

If you step into the foreach loop with the debugger, you'll find that each time through the foreach loop, the GetEnumerator method of the linked list is called, and each time through the next member in the array, it is yielded back to the calling foreach loop.

What about...

...implementing the GetEnumerator method on a more complex data structure, such as our original LinkedList?

That is shown in the next lab.

Where can I learn more?

For more on this subject, see the extensive article in MSDN titled "Iterators (C#)."

Implement GetEnumerator with Complex Data Structures

To add an iterator to your original LinkedList class, you'll implement IEnumerable<T> on both LinkedList and the Node class:

```
public class LinkedList<T> : IEnumerable<T>
public class Node<T> : IComparable<Node<T>>, IEnumerable<Node<T>>
```

How do I do that?

As noted in the previous lab, the IEnumerable interface requires that you implement only one method, GetEnumerator, as shown in Example 1-5. (Changes from Example 1-3 are highlighted.)

Example 1-5. Enumerating through your linked list

```
using System;
using System.Collections.Generic;

namespace GenericEnumeration
{
    public class Pilgrim : IComparable<Pilgrim>
    {
        private string name;
        public Pilgrim(string name)
        {
            this.name = name;
        }
        public override string ToString()
```

Example 1-5. Enumerating through your linked list (continued)

```
    {
        return this.name;
    }

    // implement the interface
    public int CompareTo(Pilgrim rhs)
    {
        return this.name.CompareTo(rhs.name);
    }
    public bool Equals(Pilgrim rhs)
    {
        return this.name == rhs.name;
    }
}


// node must implement IComparable of Node of T
// node now implements IEnumerable allowing its use in a foreach loop
public class Node<T> : IComparable<Node<T>>, IEnumerable<Node<T>> where T:
IComparable<T>
{
    // member fields
    private T data;
    private Node<T> next = null;
    private Node<T> prev = null;

    // constructor
    public Node(T data)
    {
        this.data = data;
    }

    // properties
    public T Data { get { return this.data; } }

    public Node<T> Next
    {
        get { return this.next; }
    }

    public int CompareTo(Node<T> rhs)
    {
        return data.CompareTo(rhs.data);
    }
    public bool Equals(Node<T> rhs)
    {
        return this.data.Equals(rhs.data);
    }
    // methods
    public Node<T> Add(Node<T> newNode)
    {
        if (this.CompareTo(newNode) > 0) // goes before me
```

Example 1-5. *Enumerating through your linked list (continued)*

```
        {
            newNode.next = this;   // new node points to me

            // if I have a previous, set it to point to
            // the new node as its next
            if (this.prev != null)
            {
                this.prev.next = newNode;
                newNode.prev = this.prev;
            }

            // set prev in current node to point to new node
            this.prev = newNode;

            // return the newNode in case it is the new head
            return newNode;
        }
        else         // goes after me
        {
            // if I have a next, pass the new node along for comparison
            if (this.next != null)
            {
                this.next.Add(newNode);
            }

            // I don't have a next so set the new node
                // to be my next and set its prev to point to me.
            else
            {
                this.next = newNode;
                newNode.prev = this;
            }

            return this;
        }
    }

    public override string ToString()
    {
        string output = data.ToString();

        if (next != null)
        {
            output += ", " + next.ToString();
        }

        return output;
    }


    // Method required by IEnumerable
    IEnumerator<Node<T>> IEnumerable<Node<T>>.GetEnumerator()
```

Example 1-5. Enumerating through your linked list (continued)

```
    {
        Node<T> nextNode = this;

        // iterate through all the nodes in the list
        // yielding each in turn
        do
        {
            Node<T> returnNode = nextNode;
            nextNode = nextNode.next;
            yield return returnNode;
        } while (nextNode != null);
    }
System.Collections.IEnumerator System.Collections.IEnumerable.GetEnumerator()
{
    throw new NotImplementedException();
}
    }        // end class

    // implements IEnumerable so that you can use a LinkedList
    // in a foreach loop
    public class LinkedList<T> : IEnumerable<T> where T : IComparable<T>
    {
        // member fields
        private Node<T> headNode = null;


        // properties
        // indexer
        public T this[int index]
        {
            get
            {
                int ctr = 0;
                Node<T> node = headNode;

                while (node != null && ctr <= index)
                {
                    if (ctr == index)
                    {
                        return node.Data;
                    }
                    else
                    {
                        node = node.Next;
                    }

                    ++ctr;
                } // end while
                throw new ArgumentOutOfRangeException();
            }    // end get
        }        // end indexer
```

Example 1-5. Enumerating through your linked list (continued)

```
    // constructor
    public LinkedList( )
    {
    }

    // methods
    public void Add(T data)
    {
        if (headNode == null)
        {
            headNode = new Node<T>(data);
        }
        else
        {
            headNode = headNode.Add(new Node<T>(data));
        }
    }
    public override string ToString( )
    {
        if (this.headNode != null)
        {
            return this.headNode.ToString( );
        }
        else
        {
            return string.Empty;
        }
    }


    // Implement IEnumerable required method
    // iterate through the node (which is enumerable)
    // and yield up the data from each node returned
    IEnumerator<T> IEnumerable<T>.GetEnumerator( )
    {
        foreach (Node<T> node in this.headNode)
        {
            yield return node.Data;
        }
    }
System.Collections.IEnumerator System.Collections.IEnumerable.GetEnumerator()
{
    throw new NotImplementedException();
}
    }


    class Program
    {
        private static void DisplayList<T>(string intro, LinkedList<T> theList)
            where T : IComparable<T>
```

Example 1-5. Enumerating through your linked list (continued)

```
    {
        Console.WriteLine(intro + ": " + theList);
    }

    // entry point
    static void Main(string[] args)
    {
        LinkedList<Pilgrim> pilgrims = new LinkedList<Pilgrim>();
        pilgrims.Add(new Pilgrim("The Knight"));
        pilgrims.Add(new Pilgrim("The Miller"));
        pilgrims.Add(new Pilgrim("The Reeve"));
        pilgrims.Add(new Pilgrim("The Cook"));
        pilgrims.Add(new Pilgrim("The Man of Law"));

        DisplayList<Pilgrim>("Pilgrims", pilgrims);

        Console.WriteLine("Iterate through pilgrims...");

        // Now that the linked list is enumerable, we can put
        // it into a foreach loop
        foreach (Pilgrim p in pilgrims)
        {
            Console.WriteLine("The pilgrim's name is " + p.ToString());
        }
    }
  }
}
```

Output:

```
Pilgrims: The Cook, The Knight, The Man of Law, The Miller, The Reeve
Iterate through pilgrims...
The pilgrim's name is The Cook
The pilgrim's name is The Knight
The pilgrim's name is The Man of Law
The pilgrim's name is The Miller
The pilgrim's name is The Reeve
```

What just happened?

The linked list implements its enumerator to call foreach on the head node (which you can do because Node also implements IEnumerable). Then you yield the data object you get back from the node:

```
IEnumerator<T> IEnumerable<T>.GetEnumerator()
{
    foreach (Node<T> node in this.headNode)
    {
        yield return node.Data;
    }
}
```

This gives Node the responsibility of iterating through the node list, which is accomplished, once again, using the yield statement in its own GetEnumerator method.

```
IEnumerator<Node<T>> IEnumerable<Node<T>>.GetEnumerator()
{
    Node<T> nextNode = this;
    do
    {
        Node<T> returnNode = nextNode;
        nextNode = nextNode.next;
        yield return returnNode;
    } while (nextNode != null);
}
```

You initialize nextNode to the current node, and then you begin your do...while loop. This is guaranteed to run at least once. returnNode is set to nextNode, and then, once that is stashed away, nextNode is set to *its* next node (that is, the next node in the list). Then you yield returnNode. Each time through you are returning the next node in the list until nextNode is null, at which time you stop.

What about...

...the fact that in LinkedList you asked for each Node<T> in headNode? Is headNode a collection?

Actually, headNode is the top node in a linked list. Because Node implements IEnumerable, the node is acting like a collection. This isn't as arbitrary as it sounds because a node acts as a collection in the sense that it can give you the next node in the list. You could redesign the linked list to make the nodes "dumber" and the list itself "smarter," in which case it would be the list's job to iterate over each node in turn.

Where can I learn more?

You can learn more about the IEnumerable<T> interface in the MSDN Help files, "Topic: IEnumerable<T>."

Simplify Your Code with Anonymous Methods

Anonymous methods allow you to define method blocks inline. In general, you can use anonymous methods anywhere you can use a delegate. This can greatly simplify registering event handlers.

How do I do that?

To see how you can use an anonymous method, follow these steps:

1. Open a new Windows application in Visual Studio .NET 2005 and call it AnonymousMethods.

2. Drag two controls onto the default form: a label and a button. Don't bother renaming them.

3. Double-click the button. You will be taken to the code page, where you will enter the following code:

```
private void button1_Click(object sender, EventArgs e)
{
    label1.Text = "Goodbye";
}
```

4. Run and test the application. Clicking the button changes the label text to Goodbye.

Anonymous methods allow you to pass a block of code as a parameter.

Great. No problem. But there is a bit of overhead here. You must register the delegate (Visual Studio 2005 did this for you), and you must write an entire method to handle the button click. Anonymous methods help simplify these tasks.

To see how this works, click the Show All Files button, as shown in Figure 1-1.

Figure 1-1. Show All Files button

Open *Form1.Designer.cs* and navigate to the delegate for button1.Click:

```
this.button1.Click += new System.EventHandler(this.button1_Click);
```

You can't replace this code without confusing the designer, but we will eliminate this line by returning to the form and clicking the lightning bolt in the Properties window, to go to the event handlers. Remove the event handler for the Click event.

If you return to *Form1.Designer.cs* you'll find that the button1.Click event handler is not registered!

Next, open *Form1.cs* and add the following line to the constructor, after the call to InitializeComponent( ):

```
this.button1.Click += delegate { label1.Text = "Goodbye";  };
```

Now you are ready to delete (or comment out) the event handler method:

```
//   private void button1_Click(object sender, EventArgs e)
//   {
//      label1.Text = "Goodbye";
//   }
```

Run the application. It should work exactly as it did originally.

Instead of registering the delegate which then invokes the method, the code for the delegate is placed inline in an *anonymous method*: that is, an inline, unnamed block of code.

What about...

...using anonymous methods in my own code?

No problem. Not only can you use anonymous methods when you initialize delegates, but also you can pass a block of code *anywhere* you might otherwise use a delegate.

...what happens if I reference local variables in my anonymous block?

Good question. This can cause quite a bit of confusion and is a natural trap to fall into, especially if you don't fully understand the consequences. C# allows local variables to be captured in the scope of the anonymous code block, and then they are accessed when the code block is executed. This can create some odd side effects, such as keeping objects around after they might otherwise have been collected.

...what about removing the handler for an event that I added with an anonymous delegate; how do I do that?

If you add an event handler with an anonymous delegate, you cannot remove it; therefore, I strongly recommend that you use anonymous delegates only for event handlers you expect to keep permanently attached.

You *can* use anonymous delegates for other requirements, such as implementing a List.Find method that takes, for example, a delegate describing the search criteria.

Where can I learn more?

On the MSDN web site, you'll find a good article touching on anonymous methods. Written by Juval Lowy, the article is titled "Create Elegant Code with Anonymous Methods, Iterators, and Partial Classes." Also, visit O'Reilly's ONDotnet.com site at *http://www.ondotnet.com/pub/a/dotnet/2004/04/05/csharpwhidbeypt1.html.*

Hide Designer Code with Partial Types

In previcus versions of C# the entire definition for a class had to be in a single file. Now, using the `partial` keyword, you can split your class across more than one file. This provides two significant advantages:

Using the partial keyword, you can split your class across more than one file.

- You can have different team members working on different parts of the class.

- Visual Studio 2005 can separate the designer-generated code from your own user code.

How do I do that?

The easiest way to see partial types at work is to examine the previous example (AnonymousMethods). Examine the declaration of the class in *Form1.cs*:

```
partial class Form1 : Form
{
    public Form1( )
    {
        InitializeComponent( );
        this.button1.Click += delegate { label1.Text = "Goodbye";  };

    }

    // private void button1_Click(object sender, EventArgs e)
    // {
    //     label1.Text = "Goodbye";
    // }
}
```

The `partial` keyword indicates that the code in this file does not necessarily represent the complete definition of this class. In fact, you saw earlier that the Visual Studio 2005 designer generated a second file, *Form1.Designer.cs*, which contains the rest of the definition:

```
namespace AnonymousMethods
{
    partial class Form1
    {
        /// <summary>
        /// Required designer variable.
        /// </summary>
        private System.ComponentModel.IContainer components = null;

        /// <summary>
        /// Clean up any resources being used.
        /// </summary>
```

```
protected override void Dispose(bool disposing)
{
    if (disposing && (components != null))
    {
        components.Dispose();
    }
    base.Dispose(disposing);
}

#region Windows Form Designer generated code
/// Designer-generated initialization code
...
#endregion

private System.Windows.Forms.Label label1;
private System.Windows.Forms.Button button1;
}
}
```

Together, these two files completely define the Form1 class, but you are spared dealing with the designer-generated code unless you need to work with it. This makes for simpler and cleaner development.

There is some "fine print" you need to be aware of in regard to using partial classes:

- All partial type definitions must be modified with the partial keyword and must belong to the same namespace and the same module and assembly.

- The partial modifier can appear only before the class, interface, and struct keywords.

- Access modifiers (public, private, etc.) must match all the partial types of the same class.

What about...

...using partial classes in my own projects?

Microsoft suggests that partial classes can allow developers to work on different aspects of a class independently. It is still too early to see what best practices will emerge; I'm inclined to think that any class that is big enough to be divided in this way is big enough to be split into two (or more) classes. For now, the primary use of partial classes is to hide the cruft created by the designer.

Where can I learn more?

Developer.com provides a good article on partial types. Visit *http://www. developer.com/net/net/article.php/2232061* for more information.

Create Static Classes

In addition to declaring methods as being static, now you also can declare classes as being static.

The purpose of a static class is to provide a set of static utility methods scoped to the name of the class, much as you see done with the Convert class in the Framework Class Library.

In C# 2.0 you can declare an entire class as being static to signal that you've scoped a set of static utility methods to that class.

How do I do that?

To create a static class, just add the static keyword before the class name and make sure your static class meets the criteria described earlier for static members. Also, note that static classes have the following restrictions:

- They can contain only static members.
- It is not legal to instantiate a static class.
- All static classes are sealed (you cannot derive them from a static class).

In addition to these restrictions, a static class cannot contain a constructor. Example 1-6 shows the proper use of a static class.

Example 1-6. Using static classes

```
#region Using directives

using System;

#endregion
```

Example 1-6. Using static classes (continued)

```csharp
namespace StaticClass
{

    public static class CupConversions
    {
        public static int CupToOz(int cups)
        {
            return cups * 8; // 8 ounces in a cup
        }
        public static double CupToPint(double cups)
        {
            return cups * 0.5;  // 1 cup = 1/2 pint
        }

        public static double CupToMil(double cups)
        {
            return cups * 237; // 237 mil to 1 cup
        }

        public static double CupToPeck(double cups)
        {
            return cups / 32; // 8 quarts = 1 peck
        }

        public static double CupToBushel(double cups)
        {
            return cups / 128; // 4 pecks = 1 bushel
        }
    }

    class Program
    {
        static void Main(string[] args)
        {
            Console.WriteLine("You might like to know that " +
                "1 cup liquid measure is equal to: ");
            Console.WriteLine(CupConversions.CupToOz(1) + " ounces");
            Console.WriteLine(CupConversions.CupToPint(1) + " pints");
            Console.WriteLine(CupConversions.CupToMil(1) + " milliliters");
            Console.WriteLine(CupConversions.CupToPeck(1) + " pecks");
            Console.WriteLine(CupConversions.CupToBushel(1) + " bushels");
        }
    }
}
```

Output:

```
You might like to know that 1 cup liquid measure is equal to:
8 ounces
0.5 pints
237 milliliters
0.03125 pecks
0.0078125 bushels
```

The `Program` class's main method makes calls on the static methods of the `CupConversions` class. Because `CupConversions` exists only to provide several helper methods, and no instance of `CupConversions` is ever needed, it is safe and clean to make `CupConversions` a static class.

What about...

...fields and properties? Can my static class have such members?

Yes, they can, but all the members (methods, fields, and properties) must be static.

Where can I learn more?

Eric Gunnerson has written an excellent article on static classes. You can find it in MSDN at *http://blogs.msdn.com/ericgu/archive/2004/04/13/ 112274.aspx.*

Express Null Values with Nullable Types

With new nullable types, you can assign value types a null value. This can be tremendously powerful, especially when working with databases where the value returned might be null; without nullable types you would have no way to express that an integer value is null, or that a Boolean is neither true nor false.

With nullable types, a value type such as bool or int can have the value null.

How do I do that?

You can declare a nullable type as follows:

```
System.Nullable<T> variable
```

Or, if you are within the scope of a generic type or method, you can write:

```
T? variable
```

Thus, you can create two `Nullable` integer variables with these lines of code:

```
System.Nullable<int> myNullableInt;
int? myOtherNullableInt;
```

You can check whether a nullable variable is null in two ways as well. You can check like this:

```
if (myNullableInt.HasValue)
```

---

or like this:

```
if (myNullableInt != null)
```

Each will return true if the myNullableInt variable is not null, and false if it is, as illustrated in Example 1-7.

Example 1-7. Nullable types

```
using System;

namespace NullableTypes
{
  public class Dog
  {
    private int age;
    public Dog(int age)
    {
      this.age = age;
    }
  }

  class Program
  {
    static void Main(string[] args)
    {
      int? myNullableInt = 25;
      double? myNullableDouble = 3.14159;
      bool? myNullableBool = null; // neither yes nor no

      // string? myNullableString = "Hello"; // not permitted
      // Dog? myNullableDog = new Dog(3);   // not permitted

      if (myNullableInt.HasValue)
      {
        Console.WriteLine("myNullableInt is " + myNullableInt.Value);
      }
      else
      {
        Console.WriteLine("myNullableInt is undefined!");
      }

      if (myNullableDouble != null)
      {
        Console.WriteLine("myNullableDouble: " + myNullableDouble);
      }
      else
      {
        Console.WriteLine("myNullableDouble is undefined!");
      }

      if ( myNullableBool != null )
      {
        Console.WriteLine("myNullableBool: " + myNullableBool);
```

Example 1-7. Nullable types (continued)

```
        }
        else
        {
            Console.WriteLine("myNullableBool is undefined!");
        }


        myNullableInt = null;      // assign null to the integer
        // int a = myNullableInt; // won't compile

        int b;
        try
        {
            b = (int)myNullableInt;  // will throw an exception if x is null
            Console.WriteLine("b: " + b);
        }
        catch (System.Exception e)
        {
            Console.WriteLine("Exception! " + e.Message);
        }

        int c = myNullableInt ?? -1;  // will assign -1 if x is null

        Console.WriteLine("c: {0}", c);

        // careful about your assumptions here
        // If either type is null, all comparisons evaluate false!
        if (myNullableInt >= c)
        {
            Console.WriteLine("myNullableInt is greater than or equal to c");
        }
        else
        {
            Console.WriteLine("Is myNullableInt less than c?");
        }

      }
    }
}
```

Output:

```
    myNullableInt is 25
    myNullableDouble: 3.14159
    myNullableBool is undefined!
    Exception! Nullable object must have a value.
    c: -1
    Is myNullableInt less than c?
```

What just happened?

Let's focus on the Main method. Five nullable types are created:

```
int? myNullableInt = 25;
double? myNullableDouble = 3.14159;
bool? myNullableBool = null; // neither yes nor no

// string? myNullableString = "Hello";
// Dog? myNullableDog = new Dog(3);
```

However, structs can be user-defined, and it's OK to use them as nullables.

The first three are perfectly valid, but you cannot create a nullable string or a nullable user-defined type (class), and thus they should be commented out.

We check whether each nullable type is null (or, equivalently, whether the HasValue property is true). If so, we print their value (or equivalently, we access their Value property).

After this the value null is assigned to myNullableInt:

```
myNullableInt = null;
```

The next line would like to declare an integer and initialize it with the value in myNullableInt, but this is not legal; there is no implicit conversion from a nullable int to a normal int. You can solve this in two ways. The first is with a cast:

```
b = (int)myNullableInt;
```

Comparison operators always return false if one value is null!

This will compile, but it will throw an exception at runtime if myNullableInt is null (which is why we've enclosed it in a try/catch block).

The second way to assign a nullable int to an int is to provide a default value to be used in case the nullable int is null:

```
int c = myNullableInt ?? -1;
```

This line reads as follows: "initialize int c with the value in myNullableInt unless myNullableInt is null, in which case initialize c to -1."

It turns out that all the comparison operators (>, <, <=, etc.) return false if either value is null. Thus, a true value can be trusted:

```
if (myNullableInt >= c)
{
    Console.WriteLine("myNullableInt is greater than or equal to c");
}
```

WARNING

Note, however, that == will return true if both arguments are null.

If the statement "myNullableInt is greater than or equal to c" displays, you know that myNullableInt is not null, nor is c, and that myNullableInt is greater than c. However, a false value cannot be trusted in the normal fashion:

```
else
{
    Console.WriteLine("Is myNullableInt less than c?");
}
```

This else clause can be reached if myNullableInt is less than c, but it can also be reached if either myNullableInt or c is null.

What about...

...Boolean null values? How are they compared to correspond to the SQL three-value Boolean type?

C# provides two new operators:

```
bool? operator &(bool? x, bool? y)
bool? operator |(bool? x, bool? y)
```

You can use these operators to create the truth table depicted in Table 1-1.

Table 1-1. Truth table for nullable Boolean operators

If x is...	And y is...	x and y evaluate to...	x|y evaluates to...
True	True	True	True
True	False	False	True
True	Null	Null	True
False	True	False	True
False	False	False	False
False	Null	False	Null
Null	True	Null	True
Null	False	False	Null
Null	Null	Null	Null

Where can I learn more?

The Visual C# Developer Center has a good article on nullable types. Visit *http://msdn.microsoft.com/vcsharp/2005/overview/language/nullabletypes/* for more information.

Access Objects in the Global Namespace

As in previous versions of C#, the namespace keyword is used to declare a scope. This lets you organize your code and prevents identifier collisions (for example, two different classes with the same name), especially when using third-party components.

The global namespace qualifier allows you to specify an identifier in the (default) global namespace rather than in the local namespace.

Any object that is not defined within a specific namespace is in the global namespace. Objects in the global namespace are available to objects in any other namespace. If a name collision occurs, however, you will need a way to specify that you want the object in the global namespace rather than in the local namespace.

How do I do that?

To access objects in the global namespace, you use the new global namespace qualifier (global::), as shown in Example 1-8.

Example 1-8. Using the global namespace

```csharp
using System;

namespace GlobalNameSpace
{
    class Program
    {
        // create a nested System class that will provide
        // a set of utilities for interacting with the
        // underlying system (conflicts with System namespace)
        public class System
        {
        }

        static void Main(string[ ] args)
        {

            // flag indicates if we're in a console app
            // conflicts with Console in System namespace
            bool Console = true;

            int x = 5;

            // Console.WriteLine(x); // won't compile - conflict with Console
            // System.Console.WriteLine(x); // conflicts with System

            global::System.Console.WriteLine(x); // works great.
            global::System.Console.WriteLine(Console);
        }
}
```

Example 1-8. Using the global namespace (continued)

```
    }
}
```

Output:

```
5
True
```

What just happened?

In this somewhat artificial example, you create a nested class that you named System and you created a local Boolean variable named Console. You have blocked access to the global System and Console identifiers, so neither of these lines will compile:

```
Console.WriteLine(x);
System.Console.WriteLine(x);
```

To designate that you want to use the System object in the global namespace, you will use the global namespace qualifier:

```
global::System.Console.WriteLine(x);
```

Notice that in the final line, the global namespace qualifier is used to access the System and Console objects in the global namespace, and the unqualified Console identifier is used to access the local Boolean value:

```
.global::System.Console.WriteLine(Console);
```

What about...

...other uses for the double-colon (::) operator?

The :: operator is the namespace alias qualifier. It always appears between two identifiers:

```
identifierOne::identifierTwo
```

If identifierOne is the global namespace, this operator is used to find identifierTwo within the global namespace. But if identifierOne is any namespace other than the global namespace, the operator serves to restrict the lookup of identifierOne.

Where can I learn more?

The global namespace qualifier is mentioned in the MSDN article "Create Elegant Code with Anonymous Methods, Iterators, and Partial Classes" by Juval Lowy, available at *http://msdn.microsoft.com/msdnmag/issues/04/ 05/c20/*.

Limit Access Within Properties

Now you can restrict the accessibility level of the set and set accessors within a property.

It is now possible to restrict the accessibility level of the get and set accessors within a property using access modifiers. Usually you would restrict access to the set accessor and make the get accessor public.

How do I do that?

Add the access modifier to either the get or the set accessor within the property, as illustrated in Example 1-9.

Example 1-9. Limiting access to property accessors

```csharp
#region Using directives

using System;
using System.Collections.Generic;
using System.Text;

#endregion

namespace LimitPropertyAccess
{
    public class Employee
    {
        private string name;
        public Employee(string name)
        {
            this.name = name;
        }
        public string Name
        {
            get { return name; }
            protected set { name = value; }
        }
        public virtual void ChangeName(string name)
        {
            // do work here to update many records
            Name = name; // access the private accessor
        }
    }
    class Program
    {
        static void Main(string[] args)
        {
            Employee joe = new Employee("Joe");
            // other work here
            string whatName = joe.Name; // works
            // joe.Name = "Bob"; // doesn't compile
            joe.ChangeName("Bob"); // works
            Console.WriteLine("joe's name: {0}", joe.Name);
```

Chapter 1: C# 2.0

Example 1-9. Limiting access to property accessors (continued)

```
        }
    }
}
```

Output:

```
    joe's name: Bob
```

What just happened?

The design of your `Employee` class calls for the string name to be private. You anticipate that one day you'll want to move this to a database field, so you resolve that all access to this field will be through a property, `Name`.

Other classes are free to access `Name`, but you do not want them to set the name directly. If they are going to change the name field, they must do so through the `ChangeName` virtual method. You anticipate that derived classes will do different work when an employee changes his name.

Thus you want to provide access to the `set` accessor to this class's methods and to methods of any class that derives from this class, but not to other classes. You accomplish this by adding the restricting access modifier `protected` to the `set` accessor:

```
    protected set { name = value; }
```

What about...

...restrictions on using access modifiers?

You cannot use these modifiers on interfaces or explicit interface member implementations. You can use them only if both `get` and `set` are included, and you can use them only on one or the other.

Further, the modifier must restrict access, not broaden it. Thus, you cannot make the property `protected` and then use a modifier to make `get` public.

Where can I learn more?

You can learn more about properties and access modifiers by reading the MSDN article on properties at *http://msdn.microsoft.com/library/ default.asp?url=/library/en-us/csref/html/vclrfPropertiesPG.asp*.

Gain Flexibility with Delegate Covariance and Contravariance

Covariance allows you to encapsulate a method with a return type that is directly or indirectly derived from the delegate's return type.

Now it is legal to provide a delegate method with a return type that is derived (directly or indirectly) from the delegate's defined return type; this is called *covariance*. That is, if a delegate is defined to return a Mammal, it is legal to use that delegate to encapsulate a method that returns a Dog if Dog derives from Mammal and a Retriever if Retriever derives from Dog which derives from Mammal.

Similarly, now it is legal to provide a delegate method signature in which one or more of the parameters is derived from the type defined by the delegate. This is called *contravariance*. That is, if the delegate is defined to take a method whose parameter is a Dog you can use it to encapsulate a method that passes in a Mammal as a parameter, if Dog derives from Mammal.

How do I do that?

Contravariance allows you to encapsulate a method with a parameter that is of a type from which the declared parameter is directly or indirectly derived.

Covariance and contravariance give you more flexibility in the methods you encapsulate in delegates. The use of both covariance and contravariance is illustrated in Example 1-10.

Example 1-10. Using covariance and contravariance

```
#region Using directives

using System;
using System.Collections.Generic;
using System.Text;

#endregion

namespace CoAndContravariance
{

    class Mammal
    {
        public virtual Mammal ReturnsMammal()
        {
            Console.WriteLine("Returning a mammal");
            return this;
        }
    }

    class Dog : Mammal
    {
```

Example 1-10. Using covariance and contravariance (continued)

```
    public Dog ReturnsDog()
    {
        Console.WriteLine("Returning a dog");
        return this;
    }

}

class Program
{

    public delegate Mammal theCovariantDelegate();
    public delegate void theContravariantDelegate(Dog theDog);


    private static void MyMethodThatTakesAMammal(Mammal theMammal)
    {
        Console.WriteLine("in My Method That Takes A Mammal");
    }

    private static void MyMethodThatTakesADog(Dog theDog)
    {
        Console.WriteLine("in My Method That Takes A Dog");
    }


    static void Main(string[] args)
    {
        Mammal m = new Mammal();
        Dog d = new Dog();

        theCovariantDelegate myCovariantDelegate =
            new theCovariantDelegate(m.ReturnsMammal);
        myCovariantDelegate();

        myCovariantDelegate =
            new theCovariantDelegate(d.ReturnsDog);
        myCovariantDelegate();

        theContravariantDelegate myContravariantDelegate =
            new theContravariantDelegate(MyMethodThatTakesADog);
        myContravariantDelegate(d);

         myContravariantDelegate =
            new theContravariantDelegate(MyMethodThatTakesAMammal);
        myContravariantDelegate(d);
    }
}
}
```

Output:

```
Returning a mammal
Returning a dog
in My Method That Takes A Dog
in My Method That Takes A Mammal
```

What just happened?

The Program class in Example 1-10 declares two delegates. The first is for a method that takes no parameters and returns a Mammal:

```
public delegate Mammal theCovariantMethod();
```

Earlier in the file you declared Dog to derive from Mammal.

In the run method, you declare an instance of Mammal and an instance of Dog:

```
Mammal m = new Mammal();
Dog d = new Dog();
```

You are ready to create your first instance of theCovariantDelegate:

```
theCovariantDelegate myCovariantDelegate =
    new theCovariantDelegate(m.ReturnsMammal);
```

This matches the delegate signature (m.ReturnsMammal() is a method that takes no parameters and returns a Mammal), so you can invoke the method through the delegate:

```
myCovariantDelegate();
```

Now you use covariance to encapsulate a second method within the same delegate:

```
myCovariantDelegate =
    new theCovariantDelegate(d.ReturnsDog);
```

This time, however, you are passing in a method (d.ReturnsDog()) that does not return a Mammal; it returns a Dog that derives from Mammal:

```
public Dog ReturnsDog()
{
    Console.WriteLine("Returning a dog");
    return this;
}
```

That is covariance at work. To see contravariance, you declare a second delegate to encapsulate a method that returns null and takes a Dog as a parameter:

```
public delegate void theContravariantDelegate(Dog theDog);
```

Your first instantiation of this delegate encapsulates a method with the appropriate return value (void) and parameter (Dog):

```
myContravariantDelegate =
    new theContravariantDelegate(MyMethodThatTakesADog);
```

You can invoke the method through the delegate. Your second use of this delegate, however, encapsulates a method that does not take a Dog as a parameter, but rather, takes a Mammal as a parameter:

```
theContravariantDelegate myContravariantDelegate =
    new theContravariantDelegate(MyMethodThatTakesAMammal);
```

MyMethodThatTakesAMammal is defined to take a Mammal, not a Dog, as a parameter:

```
private void MyMethodThatTakesAMammal(Mammal theMammal)
{
    Console.WriteLine("in My Method That Takes A Mammal");
}
```

Again, this works because a Dog *is a* Mammal and contravariance allows you to make this substitution.

Notice that with contravariance, you can pass in an object of the base type as a parameter where an object of the derived type is expected.

What about...

...contravariance? I get why with covariance I can return a Dog (a Dog is a Mammal), but why does contravariance work the other way? Shouldn't it accept a derived type when it expects a base type?

Contravariance is consistent with Postel's Law: "Be liberal in what you accept, and conservative in what you send." As the client, you must make sure that what you send to the method will work with that method, but as the implementer of the method you must be liberal and accept the Dog in any form, even as a reference to its base class.

Dr. Jonathan Bruce Postel (1943–1998), contributor to Internet Standards.

...what about reversing the usage of covariance and returning a base type where a derived type is expected? Can I do that?

No, it works in only one direction. You can, however, return a derived type where a base type is expected.

...what about reversing the usage of contravariance and passing in a derived type where a base type is expected?

You can't do that, either. Again, it works in only one direction. You can, however, pass in a base type where a derived type is expected.

Where can I learn more?

Internet newsgroups contain numerous discussions about the advantages and disadvantages of object-oriented languages that support covariance and contravariance. For details about using covariance and contravariance in C# programs, see the MSDN Help file pages for the two topics.

CHAPTER 2

Visual Studio 2005

The Visual Studio 2005 IDE offers a number of new productivity features, including enhancements to the Visual Studio editor, pretested code snippets, enhanced IntelliSense, and significant help with creating and organizing your code. This chapter will explore the most useful and powerful of these changes.

Configure and Save Your Developer Environment

Visual Studio 2005 is designed to enable extensive customization. For instance, you can control which tool windows are shown and how they are laid out, the placement and naming of menu commands, shortcut key combinations, help filters, and so forth.

You are encouraged to set up your development environment to match your own programming style. You can save these settings and bring them to other development machines, allowing you to have the same development environment settings on all the machines you work on. In addition, a team can share consistent settings, reducing confusion and simplifying code maintenance.

How do I do that?

After you install Visual Studio 2005, the first time you open the program you are asked to choose a configuration. The configuration you choose is saved, along with any adjustments you make later to the IDE's look and feel, in a file named *currentsettings.vssetting*. Changes to your settings are saved for you automatically in that same file.

The default location for the settings file is *[…]visual studio\settings\currentsettings.vssettings*, but you can change that location by selecting Tools → Options and then selecting Help/Import and Export Settings. There you will find a text box and a button that will open a disk browser.

You can also export your settings to a configuration file to bring to another computer by choosing Tools → Import/Export Settings. The Import and Export Settings Wizard opens, asking if you want to export selected settings, import settings, or reset all your settings to one of the default collections, as shown in Figure 2-1.

Figure 2-1. The Import and Export Settings Wizard

Once you select that you want to export settings, you are prompted to choose which settings you want to export. The wizard points out which of those setting changes might have security implications, as shown in Figure 2-2.

Note that each category has a plus sign; you can open the category and pick and choose which settings to export, as shown in Figure 2-2.

The next step is to name your settings file (the wizard suggests a name) and to choose an export location, as shown in Figure 2-3.

When you click Finish the file is saved. Now you are free to copy the file to another machine, and import it.

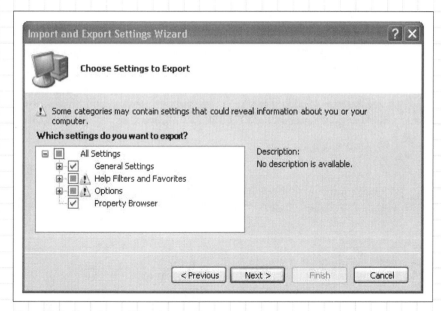

Figure 2-2. Choosing settings to export

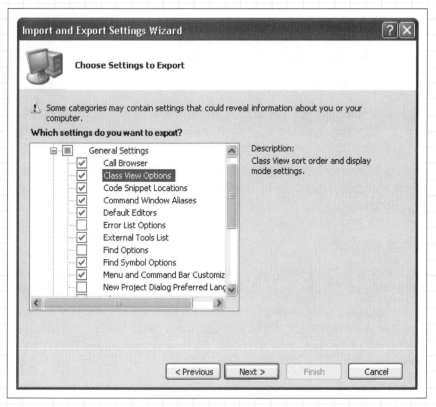

Figure 2-3. Naming your export settings file and choosing an export location

Importing the settings you saved

On the new machine, select Tools → Import/Export Settings once again. The wizard intervenes, asking if you want to save your current settings (and if so, where) or if you want to just overwrite them, as shown in Figure 2-4.

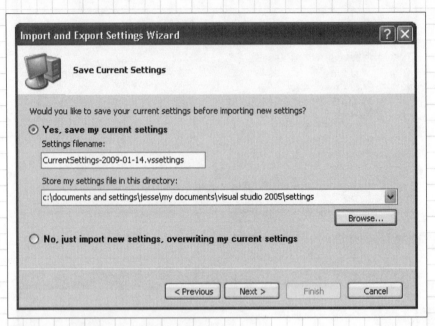

Figure 2-4. Saving settings before importing

Click Next and you are asked which collection of settings you want to import (this matches the collection you chose when you first started Visual Studio 2005), as shown in Figure 2-5.

Highlight one set of strings and click Next. That imports the strings, which you can then adjust by selecting Tools → Options, just as you could your old settings.

What about...

...specifying that all members of my team are to use the same settings for the editor, but are free to choose their own settings for the debugger?

In the Import/Export dialog box, create a unique *.vsssettings* file that specifies settings for the editor, but not other parts of Visual Studio. You do this by exporting only the Text Editor settings under the Tools → Option section.

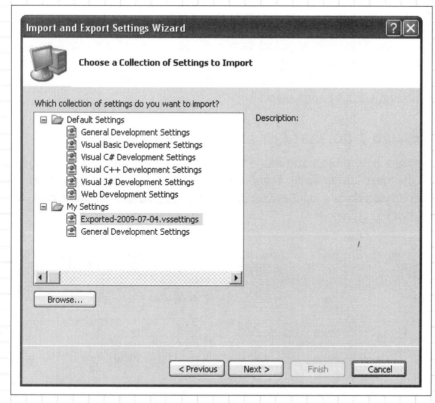

Figure 2-5. Choosing a collection to import

When the file is imported, its settings will override only the settings for the editor. All other settings will be unaffected.

...what happens if I want to provide a single *.vsssettings* file to be used by many computers?

In this case, save the settings file to a folder on your network (or just copy the file from machine to machine). Then import the settings to every computer.

Where can I learn more?

The Visual Studio 2005 Help files contain lots of information about controlling your environment settings. You can also learn a great deal just by clicking Tools → Options and poking around in the settings windows, paying particular attention to the changes in the Windows Form Designer (which, for example, defaults to layout mode) and the new tools in the Toolbox.

Configure Your Application

A number of properties affect how your program will be compiled and run. These settings are important, and when you need to change them you want to be able to find them easily. Now you can set all your application properties in one place.

How do I do that?

Create a new project and name it SimplifyCoding (you'll use this project in the next lab as well). Right-click the project and click Properties. A properties window opens with numerous tabs on the lefthand side, as shown in Figure 2-6.

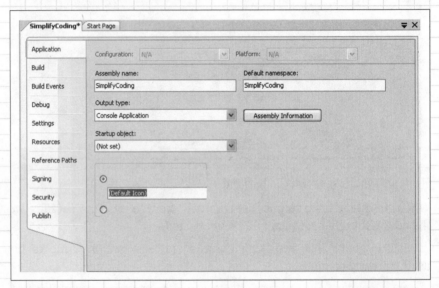

Figure 2-6. Project properties

As you click through the tabs you'll see you have immediate access to all the properties that affect how your project is built, debugged, and distributed. The final tab, Publish, can greatly simplify the work required in setting up your program for distribution, as shown in Figure 2-7.

What just happened?

When you clicked the Publish tab you were offered the opportunity to publish your application (once built) to a specific URL (for distribution over the Web) as well as the ability to set the version number. The tab also

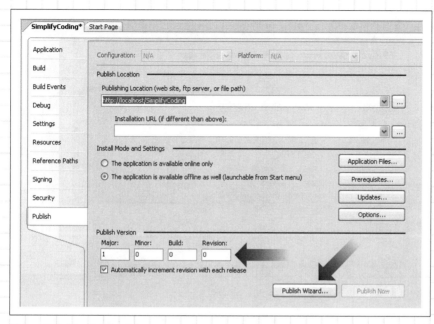

Figure 2-7. The Publish tab

includes a button to open the Publish Wizard, which walks you through the necessary setup steps to publish your fully developed application.

What about...

...publishing via an FTP server or using settings other than the default settings shown in the properties dialog?

To do this, click the Publish Wizard button shown at the bottom of Figure 2-7. Here's where you can easily modify these settings, guided by the wizard to ensure that you get the syntax right, as shown in Figure 2-8.

Where can I learn more?

The Visual Studio 2005 Help file has an extensive topic on project properties, walking you through each property individually and explaining what it does and its possible legal values.

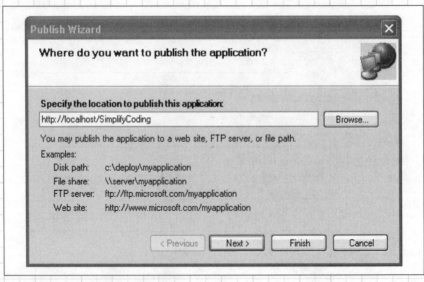

Figure 2-8. Publishing to settings you choose

Make the Editor Work for You

The Visual Studio editor can be your most important tool for creating programs.

The editor can be your most important tool for creating programs, yet few developers take the time to fully master it; and thus they miss out on potential gains in their productivity.

In this lab, you'll see how Visual Studio 2005 and several new features can work for you.

How do I do that?

The best way to explore the editor is to open a new Windows project. Let's call it EditorExploration. Visual Studio starts you out with a nice clean form named *Form1*, and also creates three additional files: *Form1.cs* to hold the code related to the form, *Form1.designer.cs* to hold the code created by the form designer, and *Program.cs* to hold the code related to the application.

Drag a label and a button anywhere onto the form, and then double-click the button to create an event handler. You should find that Visual Studio 2005 has opened a code-behind file named *Form1.cs* and has placed you inside the designer-generated button1_Click method.

Change your code

Make some minor changes to the code in your editor. Notice the yellow strip down the side of the window. This indicates changes to your code that have not yet been saved. When the changes are saved, this strip turns green.

A yellow strip indicates unsaved changes. A green strip indicates changes that have been saved.

Use IntelliSense to complete your statement

Inside the `button1_click` method, type the letter **l** (lowercase L). IntelliSense leaps to the *label1* member, which is just what you want. Insert a period (**.**) and IntelliSense will fill in the name *label1* and open up all the public methods, properties, and so forth for that control.

TIP

By default, IntelliSense leaps to the member you are most likely to want to use (often determined by remembering the member you used most recently). You can turn this off in Tools → Options → Text Editor → C# → IntelliSense. Just unclick "IntelliSense pre-selects most frequently used members."

Now you can scroll to *Text* or you can start typing (**te**...), and IntelliSense will find *Text* for you. Pressing the Tab key will complete the word once it is found (it also will set the correct capitalization).

Find compile errors before you compile

Notice the red squiggle after the word *Text.* As in Visual Studio 2002 and 2003, the red squiggle warns of a parsing error, but now IntelliSense help is available to suggest how you can fix it. Hover your mouse pointer over the squiggle, and you will see a tool tip that suggests how to fix the error. In this case it says you want a semicolon, which of course you *do not* want, but much of the time it does provide a good clue as to how to fix the problem. Complete your statement as follows:

```
label1.Text = "Goodbye";
```

Use bookmarks to simplify navigation

In previous versions of Visual Studio you used bookmarks to mark lines of source code that you return to frequently. Visual Studio 2005 includes a Bookmark Navigation window that allows you to see and manipulate all your bookmarks by renaming them as well as enabling, disabling, and removing them. The Bookmark Navigation window also allows you to move among your bookmarks and to group them into folders of bookmarks.

As with earlier versions of Visual Studio, you place a bookmark on a line of code by positioning your mouse cursor on the line and choosing Edit → Bookmarks → Toggle Bookmark, by using the shortcut key combination, or (easiest) by just clicking the Bookmark button on the toolbar, as show in Figure 2-9.

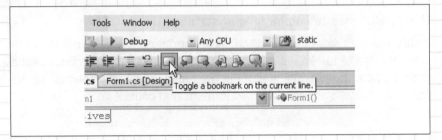

Figure 2-9. Clicking the Bookmark button

To try this feature out, double-click Program.cs and place a bookmark on a line of code in that file as well. You can move through your bookmarks most easily by clicking the Next and Previous Bookmark buttons, which are next to the Bookmark Toggle button or you may open the Bookmark window (View → Bookmark window), as shown in Figure 2-10.

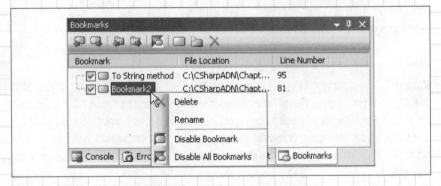

Figure 2-10. The Bookmark Navigation window

Another fast way to navigate among bookmarks is to open the Bookmarks window by selecting View → Bookmarks Window.

Dock windows where you want them

While you are in the editor, drag one of the windows from its docked position. As soon as you begin to move the window around, the docking diamond appears, as seen in Figure 2-11.

As you move the window, the four arrows of the docking diamond point to where you can dock the window. If you place your cursor over one of the arrows, the arrow darkens and you can preview the window's placement. If the window can join a tabbed group, the center of the diamond

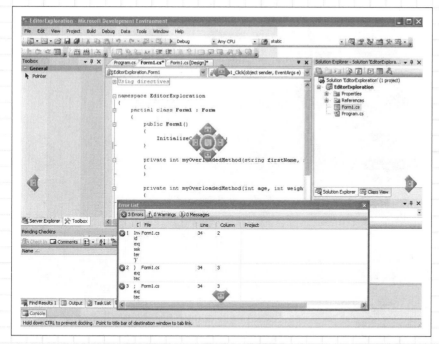

Figure 2-11. Docking a window

darkens as you pass your cursor over it. Hover your cursor over the dark-
ened center, release, and presto! Your window is tabbed.

Simplify actions with smart tags

Before we leave this lab, let's return to Design view and drag
DataGridView from the Data tab on the Toolbox onto the form. As soon as
you do, an Actions smart tag opens, as shown in Figure 2-12.

The Actions smart tag provides instant access to many of the most common actions you might want to take on this control, such as setting the
format of the grid, setting a data source, editing or adding columns in the
grid, and determining which actions will be allowed within the rows of
the grid. This is a powerful supplement to the properties window, and
makes working with the tools in the Toolbox much easier. Most controls
have a smart tag; but the decision as to whether to have one is determined by the creator of the control.

*To create a
tabbed window,
click the center of
the docking
diamond.*

What about...

...the hundreds of other nifty features in the editor?

I've added an arrow to Figure 2-12 to show you the smart tag drop-down button. When the smart tag is closed, clicking this button will reopen the smart tag.

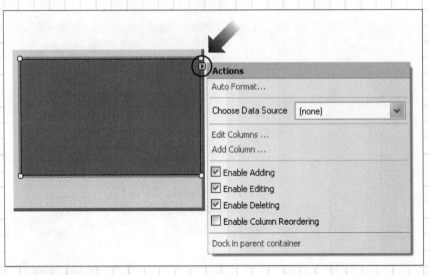

Figure 2-12. A smart tag

The truth is that one could write a book just on the programming assistance the editor provides. In the next couple of labs we'll look at some of the more powerful features, including refactoring and the use of code snippets.

Where can I learn more?

Good information about the code editor is available in the Help files, but the most powerful way to learn about the editor is to spend time playing in the editor and right-clicking various things to see what options are made available.

Use Refactoring to Speed Revision of Your Code

For most of us mortal programmers, the first version of complex code we create is not always the best it can be. As we code, we often decide to change the names of variables, factor out common routines into methods, and encapsulate member variables into properties. Some of these tasks can lead to difficulties: for example, changing the name of a variable can create subtle bugs if you forget to update references to the variable throughout the code.

Visual Studio 2005 offers a number of refactoring features that automate this process and ensure that the code is left in a consistent state.

How do I do that?

To learn more about the new refactoring features in Visual Studio 2005, first create a new Console application and name it SimplifyCoding. Replace the code provided by Visual Studio 2005 with the code shown in Example 2-1.

Example 2-1. Starting code for SimplifyCoding example

```csharp
#region Using directives

using System;
using System.Collections.Generic;
using System.Text;

#endregion

namespace SimplifyCoding
{

    public class Dog
    {
        public int age;
        public int weight;

        public Dog(int age, int weight)
        {
            this.age = age;
            this.weight = weight;
        }

        public void Method1( )
        {
            Console.WriteLine("This dog is overweight");
        }

        public void Method2(int x)
        {
            weight += x;
            Console.WriteLine("This dog is overweight");
        }


        public override string ToString( )
        {
            return "I weigh " + weight + " and I'm " + age + " years old";
        }

    }

    class Program
    {
```

Example 2-1. Starting code for SimplifyCoding example (continued)

```
static void Main(string[ ] args)
{
    Dog d = new Dog(5, 50);
    Console.WriteLine(d);
    d.weight = 70;
    Console.WriteLine(d);
    d.Method1( );
    d.Method2(35);
}

    }
}
```

WARNING

Before you run this program in the debugger, be sure to go to Tools →
Options, click Debugging/General, and check the box marked "Redirect all console output to the Quick Console Window." This will let you
see the results of your Console application within the debugger.

This is a grossly exaggerated example of a very badly written program,
but it serves to illustrate how the editor can help you improve your code.
Reading through the code as written, it is hard to know what it is supposed to do because the variables and methods are poorly named. In
addition, this code might be hard to maintain because some blocks of
code are repeated in more than one place. This is always dangerous
because it is easy to modify one block and neglect to update the other. In
addition, this code exposes public member variables, a process that
breaks down encapsulation and can cause maintenance headaches if you
later change how you store the data held by those members (for example, if you later decide to store the dog's age and weight in a database,
you'll break any class that interacts with these members of the Dog class).

We'll improve this code by renaming the variables and methods, by fac-
toring out common code, and by encapsulating what are currently public
member variables. All of these tasks are made much easier (and safer) by
the new refactoring support offered in Visual Studio 2005.

Let's do this step by step.

Change a method name

Though the name doesn't tell you so, the job of Method1 is to see if the dog
is overweight. Right now, that is stubbed out (it displays the message "This
dog is overweight"). Begin by renaming Method1 to TestDogOverweight. As

you type the new name, you'll see an orange bar under the name, as shown in Figure 2-13.

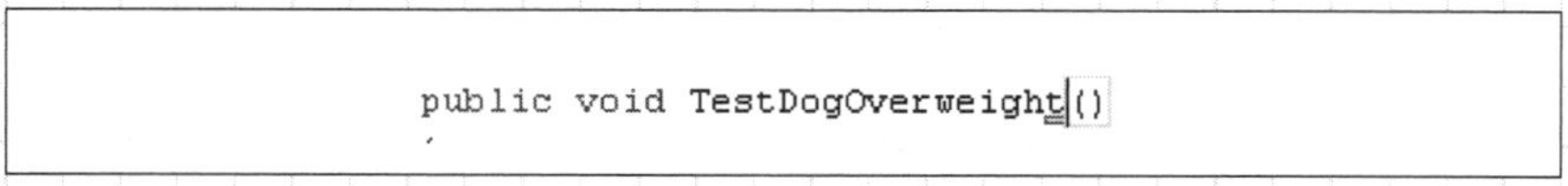

```
public void TestDogOverweight()
```

Figure 2-13. The bar that appears when you change an identifier

Click the bar and a smart tag appears offering to change the name of your method, as shown in Figure 2-14.

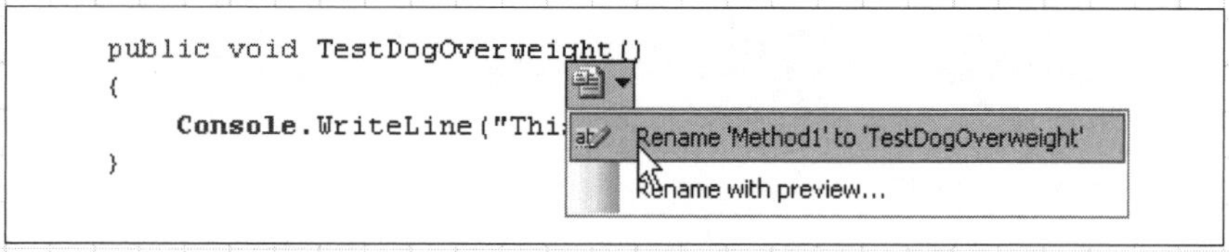

```
public void TestDogOverweight()
{
    Console.WriteLine("Thi:|  Rename 'Method1' to 'TestDogOverweight'
}                             Rename with preview...
```

Figure 2-14. A smart tag for changing an identifier

Click Rename 'Method1' to 'TestDogOverweight' and you'll find that the name is changed in the method, as well as everywhere the method is called! Very nice. Add the following lines to TestDogOverweight:

```
Console.WriteLine("Need to walk the dog");
Console.WriteLine("Get Leash");
Console.WriteLine("Go for walk");
weight--;
```

Change a parameter name

Method2 and its parameter x would also benefit from a name change. Rename Method2 to FeedDog and rename x to howMuchFood. In each case a smart tag appears, and by using the smart tag to complete the renaming, the identifier is renamed throughout your code. Replace the Writeline statement in this method with a call to TestDogOverweight:

```
public void FeedDog(int howMuchFood)
{
    weight += howMuchFood;
    TestDogOverweight();
}
```

Add a new method, to awaken the dog in the morning:

```
public void AwakenDog()
{
    Console.WriteLine("WakeDogUp");
    Console.WriteLine("Get Leash");
    Console.WriteLine("Go for walk");
    weight--;
}
```

Factor out methods

Notice that the last three lines in this new method are identical to the last three lines in TestDogOverweight. Let's factor these lines out to a method. Highlight the three lines and right-click. Choose Refactor → ExtractMethod. The ExtractMethod dialog appears. Name the new method WalkDog and press Enter. Hey! Presto! A new private helper method is created called WalkDog with the three lines of code, and in the place from which you extracted the method you find a call to your new method!

```
public void AwakenDog( )
{
   Console.WriteLine("WakeDogUp");
   Console.WriteLine("Need to walk the dog");
   WalkDog( );
}
private void WalkDog( )
{
   Console.WriteLine("Get Leash");
   Console.WriteLine("Go for walk");
   weight--;
}
```

Now you can go to your first method and make a call to WalkDog there, thus simplifying your code and ensuring maintainability.

Protect a field

Finally, notice that the Run method in Tester accesses the dog's weight directly:

```
d.weight = 70;
```

This works because weight is (improperly) declared to be a public member variable. We'd like to refactor all public member variables into properties. Highlight the definition of weight in the dog class and right-click. Choose Refactor → Encapsulate Field. The Encapsulate Field dialog comes up and offers to name the property with a capital letter and to update references to the property, as shown in Figure 2-15.

Notice that you have two choices for updating references. You can update only external references (references from methods outside of this class), or you can update all references. Choose External, click OK, and you can preview the changes that are about to take place. Click OK again, and the public variable is fully encapsulated as a property:

```
private int weight;
public int Weight
{
   get
   {
```

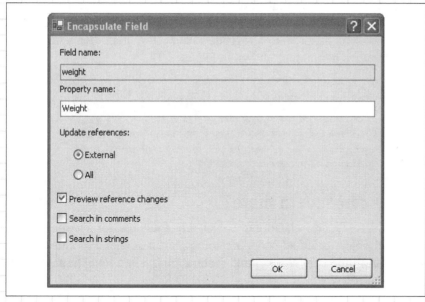

Figure 2-15. Encapsulating a field

```
        return weight;
    }

    set
    {
        weight = value;
    }
}
```

What about...

...if I want only a get method?

Although the property encapsulation creates a get and a set method, you can implement only a get method. It's just code in the editor. Once the code that implements the change is created, you are free to edit it in any way you want, including eliminating set accessors (though doing so might break your existing program if you accessed the variable from outside the class).

...what about other refactoring tasks that are available in the C# editor?

The C# editor offers quite a few tasks, including tasks for extracting an interface, promoting a local variable to a parameter, removing parameters, and reordering parameters.

...what about exploring further improvements to Visual Studio 2005?

One of my favorites is that now when you choose Find All References, you get a *list* of the references to the defined term. Then you can click each reference and go to the code where the item (for example, a method call) is defined, as shown in Figure 2-16.

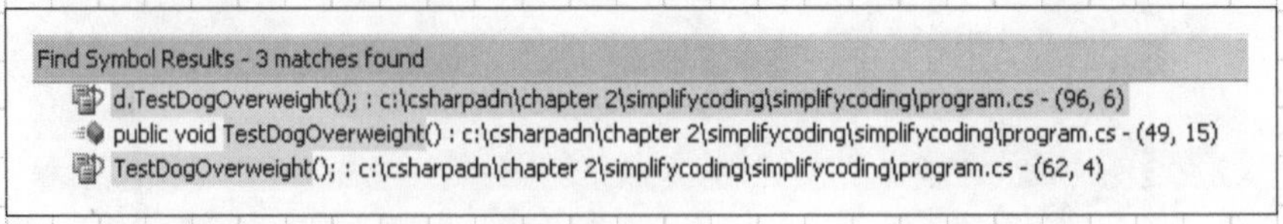

Find Symbol Results - 3 matches found

d.TestDogOverweight(); : c:\csharpadn\chapter 2\simplifycoding\simplifycoding\program.cs - (96, 6)
public void TestDogOverweight() : c:\csharpadn\chapter 2\simplifycoding\simplifycoding\program.cs - (49, 15)
TestDogOverweight(); : c:\csharpadn\chapter 2\simplifycoding\simplifycoding\program.cs - (62, 4)

Figure 2-16. Finding all references to a method

Where can I learn more?

A number of good refactoring books are available for creating well-designed object-oriented code, including Martin Fowler's seminal classic *Refactoring* (Addison-Wesley) and Joshua Kerievsky's *Refactoring to Patterns* (Addison-Wesley).

Use Code Snippets to Save Typing

There are a number of patterns that you use all the time (for example, for statements).Visual Studio 2005 makes it easy to insert these in your code.

How do I do that?

For example, returning to the previous lab, say you want to add some conditional code to actually test if the dog is overweight. Begin by high-lighting the code within the TestDogOverweight method, and then right-click it. Choose Surround With: and the Surround With menu pops up, as shown in Figure 2-17.

Choose the if statement (be careful not to choose #if), and an if block is created around your block of code. The if condition is initialized true and is highlighted for you to type in new code. IntelliSense helps you complete the code, as shown in Figure 2-18.

What just happened?

With a couple of keystrokes, you were able to surround a block of code with a well-formed if statement. The variables used in the if statement

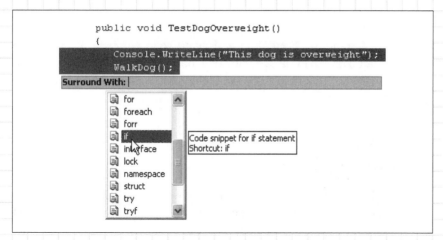

Figure 2-17. The Surround With menu with the if statement highlighted

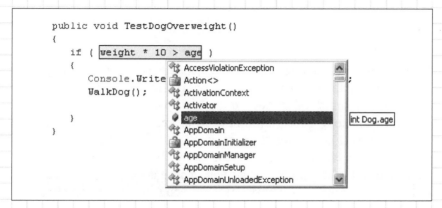

Figure 2-18. Filling in the if statement

were offered by IntelliSense, enabling you to make sure you used the correct spelling and capitalization.

What about...

...using expansions without surrounding existing code?

Rather than using expansion surround, just use the code expansion snippet. The expansions in IntelliSense allow you to quickly create any of a wide variety of coding structures. For example, if you just type the word foreach followed by a tab, a foreach loop is created with each editable field highlighted in yellow. You can tab through the fields with the Tab key, and when you are done, pressing Enter or Esc will return the editor to normal.

Where can I learn more?

For more information on creating and using code snippets, keep an eye on GODotnet.com. Over time users will be creating code snippets that you'll be able to import into Visual Studio 2005 to expand your repertoire of reusable code.

Examine Objects While Debugging Them

Now you can peer inside complex objects. It's MRI for programmers.

In Visual Studio 2005 you can look inside complex objects, including user-defined classes and collections, right from within the editor. You do so by hovering your mouse cursor over the object while in debug mode. This is the same as in previous versions of Visual Studio, but the amount of information provided is much greater than before.

How do I do that?

To see an example of how to look at the state of complex objects, place a breakpoint on the last line of the SimplifyCoding program shown in Example 2-1. Run the debugger to the breakpoint and place your cursor over the variable d, which represents an instance of Dog. Notice that the text that would be rendered by calling ToString on the Dog object is shown, just as in previous versions. Now, however, a plus sign (+) appears next to the variable. Hover your mouse cursor over the plus sign; the plus sign turns to a minus sign, and you'll see the internals of the instance, as shown in Figure 2-19.

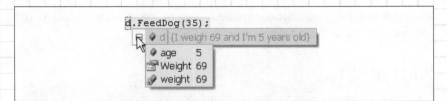

Figure 2-19. Looking inside objects

What about...

...seeing other types of data such as XML or datasets?

The debugger comes with built-in visualizers for text, HTML, and XML. You are also free to create your own. The next lab examines how to use the XML Visualizer.

Where can I learn more?

A number of good books on using debuggers are available, including the seminal work *Code Complete* by Steve McConnell (Microsoft Press).

Visualize XML Data

As noted in the previous lab, the debugger allows you to examine text, HMTL, and XML. In this lab you'll create an XML document, read it into a program, and then examine the XML data using the XML Visualizer.

Visual Studio 2005 provides an XML Visualizer for examining XML data.

How do I do that?

Create a new Console application named ExamineXML. Add an XML file to the project by right-clicking the project and choosing Add → New Item → XML File. Name the new XML file *BookList.xml* and populate it with the valid XML data shown in Example 2-2.

Example 2-2. Valid XML data sample

```xml
<?xml version="1.0" ?>
<Books>
    <book>
        <BookName>Programming C#</BookName>
        <Author>Jesse Liberty</Author>
        <Publisher>O'Reilly Media</Publisher>
    </book>
    <book>
        <BookName>Programming ASP.NET</BookName>
        <Author>Jesse Liberty</Author>
        <Author>Dan Hurwitz</Author>
        <Publisher>O'Reilly Media</Publisher>
    </book>
    <book>
        <BookName>Visual C# Notebook</BookName>
        <Author>Jesse Liberty</Author>
        <Publisher>O'Reilly Media</Publisher>
    </book>
</Books>
```

Next, write a Test method to read the XML file using a StreamReader object and concatenate all the strings read into a single long XML string, as shown in Example 2-3.

Example 2-3. Reading the XML file

```csharp
using System;
using System.IO;
using System.Xml;
```

Example 2-3. Reading the XML file (continued)

```
namespace ExamineXML
{
    class Program
    {
        static void Main(string[ ] args)
        {
            using (StreamReader reader = File.OpenText(@"..\..\BookList.xml"))
            {
                string completeXML = reader.ReadToEnd( );
                Console.WriteLine("Received: {0}", completeXML);
            }


        }
    }
}
```

Place a breakpoint on the last line of the Main method. When you hit the breakpoint, hover your mouse cursor over the complete XML string. The string will be shown, and at the end of the display will be a magnifying glass. Click the magnifying glass and you'll have the opportunity to pick the Visualizer you want to use, as shown in Figure 2-20 (the arrow in Figure 2-20 points to the magnifying glass).

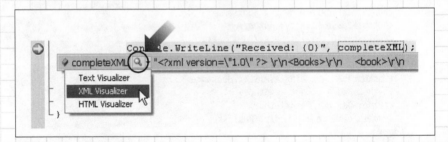

Figure 2-20. Picking the Visualizer

You can examine the complete string in the debugger using either the Text Visualizer or, more interestingly, the XML Visualizer, as shown in Figure 2-21.

WARNING

The XML Visualizer will not work as shown if encoding = "utf-8" is specified in the XML file.

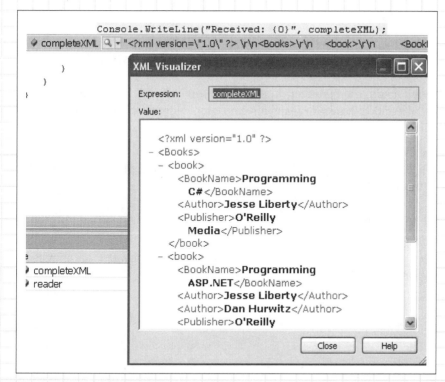

Figure 2-21. The XML Visualizer

What about...

...custom (proprietary) data?

The framework provides you with classes to enable you to create your own visualizers. To see how, read the MSDN article "How to: Create a Debugger Visualizer Using Visual Studio 2005."

Where can I learn more?

Run a search in Google with the words "Visual Studio Visualizer." When I ran that search I found more than 700 hits, many of which were projects that demonstrated how to create new visualizers, such as image visualizers. This is a rapidly emerging technology.

Diagnose Exceptions

The new Exception Assistant gives you a strong head start on figuring out why your code threw an exception and what to do about it.

How do I do that?

The new Visual Studio 2005 Exception Assistant is always turned on; you don't have to do anything special (except for throwing an exception) to call it into action. When an exception is thrown, the editor switches to Break mode, the statement that caused the exception is highlighted, and the Exception Assistant leaps forward with suggestions for what to do.

The Exception Assistant helps you diagnose why an exception was thrown.

To see this at work, go back to ExamineXML, the project you created for the "Visualize XML Data" lab, and in the source code change the name of the file to be read by StreamReader from *BookList.xml* to *BadFileName.xml*, a nonexistent file:

```
// using (StreamReader reader = File.OpenText(@"..\..\BookList.xml"))
using (StreamReader reader = File.OpenText(@"..\..\BadFileName.xml"))
```

Run the program by pressing F5. The code will break on the line you've changed, and the Exception Assistant will come forward, as shown in Figure 2-22.

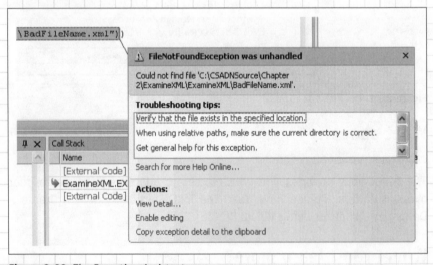

Figure 2-22. The Exception Assistant

At this point, you can click one of the Troubleshooting Tips to open the appropriate Help file page, or you can click View Detail.

In this case, the problem is self-evident; the file could not be found, and your job is only to figure out why the OpenText method could not find your file.

What about...

...the View Detail link? What is that for?

Clicking the View Detail link will open the View Detail dialog box, as shown in Figure 2-23.

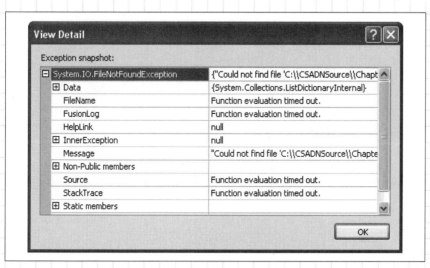

Figure 2-23. The View Detail dialog box

The details in this particular case are not very helpful because the exception is self-explanatory, but for some types of head-banging exceptions, the Exception Snapshot panel of the View Detail window can provide the information you need.

Where can I learn more?

C# Corner has a good article on exception handling at *http://www.c-sharpcorner.com/Tutorials/ExceptionHandling101RVS.asp*, as does O'Reilly's ONDotnet.com site at *http://www.ondotnet.com/pub/a/dotnet.2001.09/04/error_handling.html*.

CHAPTER 3

Windows Applications

.NET 2.0 adds a host of rich controls that make it easier than ever to build Windows clients and to cut down on coding. Among the new controls we will examine in this chapter are those that provide improved menus and tool strips, masked edit controls, and a built-in web browser control. You'll also learn how to put ClickOnce deployment, a new Microsoft technology for deploying Windows clients, to work.

Add Tool Strips to Your Application

.NET 2.0 introduces a new ToolStrip control that provides a modern Office look for toolbars, handles Windows themes, and provides access through the toolbar to a plethora of controls, including buttons, lists, menus, labels, and more.

How do I do that?

To get started, open a new Windows application and call it Toolbars. Make sure the Toolbox is open and drag a ToolStripContainer control onto your form. Click the ToolStripContainer smart tag for a list of ToolStripContainer tasks. The ToolStripContainer control allows you to specify that the panel be visible at the top, bottom, left, or right of the application Window, as shown in Figure 3-1. Choose top only.

Drag a ToolStrip control from the Toolbox onto the ToolStripContainer control, and click the smart tag to open the ToolStrip Tasks menu. Click Insert Standard Items to add the standard tool strip items, as shown in Figure 3-2.

In this chapter:
- *Add Tool Strips to Your Application*
- *Allow Valid Input Only*
- *Create Auto-Complete Text Boxes*
- *Play Sounds*
- *Create Split Windows*
- *Create Data-Driven Forms*
- *Create Safe Asynchronous Tasks*
- *Put the Web in a Window*
- *Enable One-Click Deployment*

The ToolStrip control helps you create modern menus with zero coding.

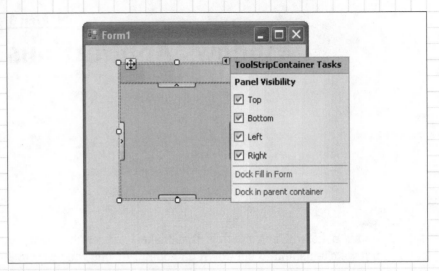

Figure 3-1. The ToolStripContainer smart tag

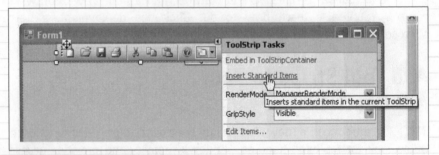

Figure 3-2. Adding a tool strip

Clicking the Edit Items option at the bottom of the ToolStrip Tasks menu opens the Items Collection Editor. This allows you to add new items to the tool strip as well as to manipulate the strip itself, setting such properties as CanOverflow, as shown in Figure 3-3.

The CanOverflow property can be set through the properties window, the smart tag, or dynamically at runtime. If you enable this property and then shrink the window so that the tool strip no longer fits, a special menu appears at the right that makes the missing buttons available, as shown in Figure 3-4.

The ToolStrip control is designed to hold a number of ToolStripItem controls, including those listed in Table 3-1.

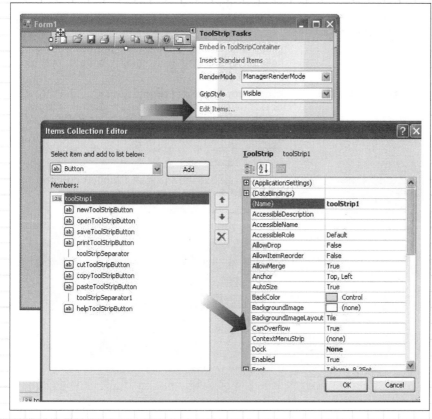

Figure 3-3. Editing the tool strip and adding items

Figure 3-4. The overflow menu

Table 3-1. ToolStripItem controls

ToolStripItem control	Description
ToolStripButton	An item the user can click. Buttons can be text, images, or both. The toolbars shown in Figure 3-4 illustrate standard buttons with images.
ToolStripLabel	An item the user cannot click. Labels can be text, images, or both.

You can use
ToolStripControl-
Host to create
your own
ToolStripItem
controls.

Table 3-1. ToolStripItem controls (continued)

ToolStripItem control	Description
ToolStripSeparator	Divides items with a thin indented line. You can see these in any standard menu. They also are shown in the toolbar in Figure 3-2.
ToolStripDropDownButton	Creates drop-down menus with items. ToolStripDropDownButton shows its items as a menu, with the ability to check items, as shown in Figure 3-5.
ToolStripSplitButton	Creates a two-part control. The left part is a standard button, and the right part is a drop-down menu, as shown in Figure 3-6.
ToolStripComboBox ToolStripTextBox ToolStripProgressBar	These are just like the equivalent Windows controls, except they derive from ToolStripControlHost.

Figure 3-5. The drop-down button

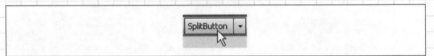

Figure 3-6. The split button

All the controls housed in a ToolStrip control derive from the ToolStripItem class, and all share the Text and Image properties, making it easy to work with each of them in a uniform way.

If you click an item in your tool strip and then click the event button in the properties window (the one with the lightening bolt) to see its associated events, you'll find that the menu item supports a variety of events. As with other, standard controls, double-clicking opens the default event (Click), making it trivial to create an event handler for clicking a ToolStrip control.

By default, each
control on a tool
strip has its own
Click event
handler.

What about...

...other controls? The look and feel of the tool strip interface is consistent with the look and feel of Office 2003. Do controls provide support for Office look and feel?

Yes, the StatusStrip, MenuStrip, and ContextMenuStrip controls also provide support for the look and feel of Office 2003.

Note that these controls replace the StatusBar, MainMenu, and ContextMenu controls of Windows Forms 1.x, in much the same way that ToolStrip replaces the old ToolBar control. You can drag a MenuStrip control into the same ToolstripContainer as the ToolStrip control, and the form will place them appropriately, with the menu bar directly above the toolbar, as shown in Figure 3-7.

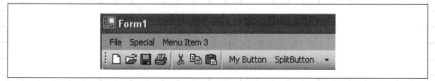

Figure 3-7. The MenuStrip added

...what if I want to get to the old Toolbar control? It isn't in my Toolbox.

To access the old versions of these controls you must manually add them to the Visual Studio Toolbox. Right-click the Toolbox and select Choose Items.... This step opens the Choose Toolbox Items dialog, where you can select the traditional ToolBar control, as shown in Figure 3-8.

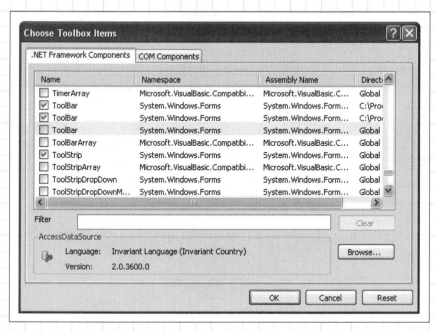

Figure 3-8. Adding the traditional ToolBar control

Where can I learn more?

You'll find extensive articles on using the new ToolStrips on the .NET Framework Windows Forms site at *http://www.windowsforms.net*.

Allow Valid Input Only

Visual Studio 2005 includes a *masked editing control* in its Toolbox—courtesy of .NET 2.0. It allows you to restrict the input from a user and control how it is displayed by using a *mask*. For example, you might want to use a telephone mask so that when a user enters **6175551212**, the mask will render the input as **(617) 555-1212**.

A mask can block invalid characters (such as %) and can signal to the user what is expected (for example, the parentheses indicate that an area code is required).

How do I do that?

Create a new Windows Forms application project, name it MaskedEntry, and drag a MaskedTextBox control to the form created by the Visual Studio Designer. Click the smart tag and choose the one action available: "Set the mask associated with the control." The Input Mask dialog opens, as shown in Figure 3-9.

The Framework provides you with preconfigured masks.

As you can see, .NET 2.0 provides you with a number of standard masks. Choose the "Phone number" mask; the mask appears in the Mask text box, and you are invited to try it out in the "Try it" text box, as shown in Figure 3-10.

If you are happy with the mask you've selected, click the OK button and the mask you selected will be associated with the Mask control, as shown in Figure 3-11.

If you click the MaskedTextBox control and examine its properties in the Properties window you'll find a few useful properties, as shown in Table 3-2.

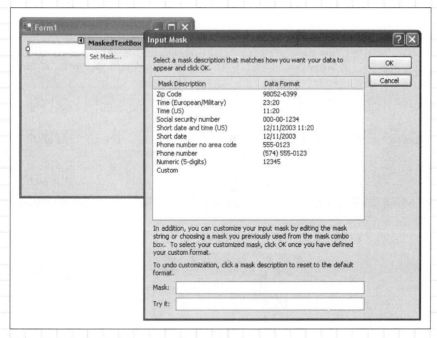

Figure 3-9. Masked text box Input Mask dialog

Figure 3-10. Trying the "Phone number" mask

Figure 3-11. A mask associated with MaskedTextBox

Table 3-2. MaskedTextBox properties

Property	Description
Mask	The mask you've chosen. If you click the ellipses, the Mask Input dialog box reopens. You are also free to type in your own custom mask.
BeepOnError	If the user types an invalid character and BeepOnError is set to true, the computer emits the standard error tone. The default is false.
PromptChar	Until the mask is filled, each missing character is replaced with this character. The default is the underscore (_).

Replacing the PromptChar default character with a question mark (?) changes the prompt character displayed in the mask, as shown in Figure 3-12.

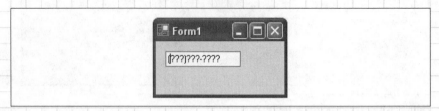

Figure 3-12. Changing the prompt character

When you interact with the MaskedTextBox control programmatically, you can test its MaskCompleted property, which returns true only if there are no empty characters in the mask.

When you want to retrieve the text from MaskedTextBox you can access the Text property.

To see this at work, add three new controls to the form, as shown in Figure 3-13:

- A checkbox (cbMaskComplete)
- A text box (txtText)
- A label control (the label for the text box)

Create an event handler for the TextChanged event on maskedTextBox1:

```
private void maskedTextBox1_TextChanged(object sender, EventArgs e)
{
    cbMaskComplete.Checked = maskedTextBox1.MaskCompleted;
    txtText.Text = maskedTextBox1.Text;
}
```

Each time you enter a character into maskedTextBox1 the other controls will be updated, as shown in Figure 3-14.

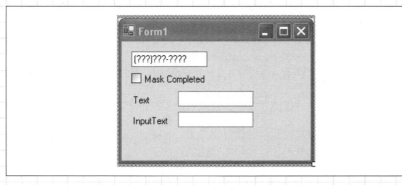

Figure 3-13. The updated mask form

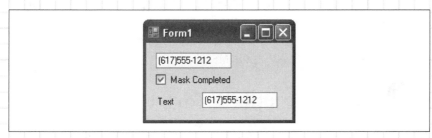

Figure 3-14. The completed mask

What about...

...creating my own mask? How do I do that?

You can create your own mask using the special mask characters shown in Table 3-3.

Table 3-3. Mask values

Character	Mask value
0 (zero)	Required digit
9	Optional digit
A	Required alphanumeric character
a	Optional alphanumeric character
&	Required Unicode character
C	Optional Unicode character
#	Optional digit or space, or plus or minus symbol
L	Required letter (a–z, A–Z)
?	Optional letter
. (period)	Decimal placeholder

Table 3-3. Mask values (continued)

Character	Mask value
, (comma)	Thousands placeholder
$	Currency symbol
: (colon)	Separate time values
/ (forward slash)	Separate date values
< (less than)	Force to lowercase
> (greater than)	Force to uppercase

Where can I learn more?

C# Corner has a nice example of using the MaskedTextBox control at *http://www.c-sharpcorner.com/Code/2004/Sept/MaskedTextBox.asp*. You can find a full description of the properties and nuances of MaskedTextBoxes in the article "MaskedTextBox Class" in the MSDN.

Create Auto-Complete Text Boxes

You can add text completion to any TextBox or ComboBox control.

When you type a URL into Internet Explorer, it attempts to help you complete the address by providing a list of addresses that match what you've typed so far. The newly updated TextBox and ComboBox controls provided with Visual Studio 2005 allow you to add that functionality to your Windows Forms as well.

How do I do that?

Create a new Windows application, call it TextComplete, and drag a TextBox onto the form.

Click the TextBox control, and in the properties window drop down the AutoCompleteMode property, as shown in Figure 3-15. (I blanked out the surrounding properties to make this easier to see.)

The three choices for AutoCompleteMode are shown in Table 3-4.

Table 3-4. AutoCompleteMode choices

Mode	Meaning
Suggest	Displays the drop-down list populated with one or more suggested completion strings
Append	Appends the remainder of the most likely candidate string (highlighted)
SuggestAppend	Combines both Suggest and Append

For `AutoCompleteMode` to work, you must specify where to get the list of suggestions. You do so in the `AutoCompleteSource` property, as shown in Figure 3-16 (again, to make the figure easier to read, I've blanked out the other properties).

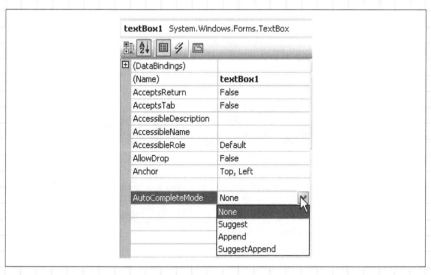

Figure 3-15. The AutoCompleteMode property

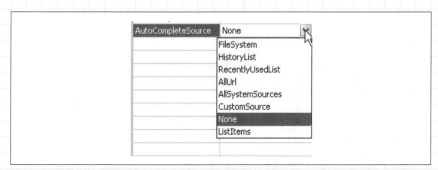

Figure 3-16. The AutoCompleteSource property

The possible values and what they indicate are listed in Table 3-5.

Table 3-5. AutoCompleteSource choices

Source	Meaning
FileSystem	Recently entered file paths.
HistoryList	Taken from Internet Explorer's history list.
RecentlyUsedList	All documents in the "most recently used list" in the Start menu.
AllURL	All sites recently visited.

Table 3-5. AutoCompleteSource choices (continued)

Source	Meaning
AllSystemSources	All URLs and all files.
CustomSources	Items in the AutoCompleteCustomSource collection that you populate either at design time or programmatically.
ListItems	Not valid with TextBox. Used with ComboBox to pick from items in the ComboBox Items collection.

Once you've filled in these properties, the list works automatically for you, as shown in Figure 3-17.

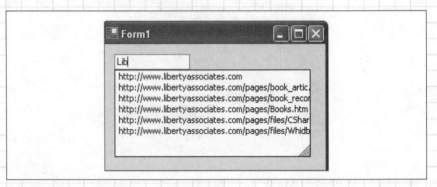

Figure 3-17. AutoCompleteMode at work

What just happened?

For the auto-complete text box in Figure 3-17, I set AutoCompleteMode to Suggest and I set AutoCompleteSource to AllUrl. You might want to try changing these settings and seeing the resulting changes in the text box.

What about...

...the word "custom" in the auto-complete enumeration? How do I create a custom source for auto-completion?

The auto-complete source must be an AutoCompleteStringCollection. You can easily create a custom source at design time by setting the AutoCompleteSource property to CustomSource and then clicking the AutoCompleteCustomSource property to fill in the string collection with whatever strings you want to appear in the drop-down list. Of course, you can set this programmatically at runtime as well.

Where can I learn more?

You can learn a bit more about the properties associated with auto-completion by checking the Help Index entry for the TextBox class.

Play Sounds

.NET 2.0 provides a new SystemSounds class that allows you to play the most common Windows system sounds with a single line of code, no matter where they are located on your operating system. In addition, the SoundPlayer control will play *.wav* files with nearly no coding.

How do I do that?

Create a new Windows application project, name it Sounds, and drag a button (button1) onto the form. Set the text of the button to System Sound (you'll have to stretch the button to make room for the words).

The new System-Sounds class allows you to play the most common system sounds with a single line of code.

TIP

Setting text in the button is not required, but it does make it easier to play with this test application.

Double-click the button and you'll go to its Click event handler. In the code stub for the event handler, type the keyword **SystemSounds** followed by a period (**.**). The list of system sounds you can play is displayed, as shown in Figure 3-18.

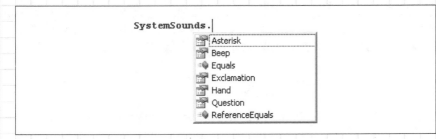

```
SystemSounds.|
        Asterisk
        Beep
        Equals
        Exclamation
        Hand
        Question
        ReferenceEquals
```

Figure 3-18. System sounds

Choose Asterisk, type a period (**.**), and then choose Play from the list presented by IntelliSense. The result is the following code:

```
SystemSounds.Asterisk.Play();
```

Run the application, and then press the button (labeled System Sound). Voila! A system sound!

To play a *.wav* file, add a SoundPlayer control to the form. It is immediately dropped into the tool panel at the bottom of the form.

You can tell this SoundPlayer control to play a *.wav* file by setting its SoundLocation property, or you can ask it to play a sound from a stream-based object (perhaps obtained over the Web) by setting its Stream property.

Add a second button (button2) to the form and set its text to "WAV File." Double-click the button, and in the event handler, add code to hardwire your SoundPlayer control to a *.wav* file on your computer, as shown in the following fragment:

```
private void button2_Click(object sender, EventArgs e)
{
    this.soundPlayer1.SoundLocation = @"C:\Windows\Media\Chimes.wav";
    this.soundPlayer1.Play();
}
```

Clearly a more elegant solution would be to provide the user with a drop-down list of .wav files to play; this is left as an exercise for the reader. Be sure to reset the location of the .wav file as appropriate for your computer.

What about...

...playing the audio synchronously and waiting for it to complete before returning control to the application?

Sure, you can do this. Instead of calling the Play method, call the PlaySync method. This will play your *.wav* file in the same thread as the application. You can also call PlayLooping, which works just like Play except that it keeps playing until you tell it to stop by calling, logically enough, Stop.

Where can I learn more?

For more information on the sound player and on playing sounds, see the MSDN Documentation article "Sound Player Class Overview."

Create Split Windows

The new SplitContainer control makes creating split windows in Windows Forms a snap. The two panels can be side by side or one on top of the other, and you can nest splitters one within another to further divide the form.

How do I do that?

Create a new Windows application, name it SplitWindows, and drag a SplitContainer control onto the form. Notice that its default orientation is to split vertically. Click the smart tag, and choose Horizontal Splitter Orientation.

Now you have two panels, top and bottom. Drag a second SplitContainer control into the bottom panel. Click in the bottom-left panel and set the background color to blue. Click in the bottom-right panel and set the background color to red. Then set the upper panel to green.

Run the application. The three panels are clearly visible, and when you pass your cursor over the divisions, the cursor changes to the splitter cursor, as shown in Figure 3-19. (I've surrounded the cursor with a white box to make it easy to find.)

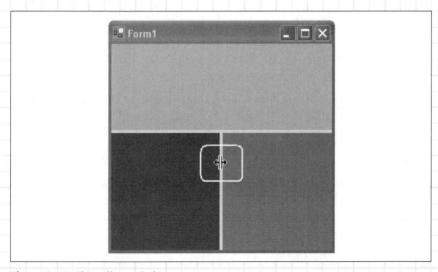

Figure 3-19. The splitter windows

When you create a SplitContainer control, its Dock property is automatically set to DockStyle.Fill. You can undo this to specify how much space you want your splitter to take up or you can prefill a portion of the form with a panel, and the splitter will take the remaining room.

If you undock the splitter, you can move it about within the form using the grab handles, as shown in Figure 3-20.

What about...

...restricting the size of the SplitContainer control?

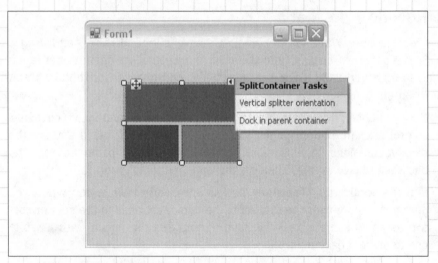

Figure 3-20. Moving the splitter

You can set the `Panel1MinSize` or `Panel2MinSize` properties to set the minimum size of each panel. You can even stop resizing altogether by setting the `IsSplitterFixed` property to `True`.

Normally, when you resize the window each panel is resized proportionally. You can override that behavior, however, by setting the `FixedPanel` property of one of the panels to `True`. In that case, that panel will hold its size when the form is resized, and the other panels will adjust accordingly.

Where can I learn more?

For more information, see the MSDN article titled "Split Containers."

Create Data-Driven Forms

FlowLayoutPanel and TableLayout-Panel make adding controls dynamically fast and easy.

One of the features that designers request most frequently of data-driven Windows Forms is the ability to add new controls to a form quickly, easily, and with a consistent layout. Visual Studio 2005 provides two new controls to help you do that: `FlowLayoutPanel` and `TableLayoutPanel`.

Each control derives from `Panel`, and each gives you a means to automate how controls are added to the panel. This is especially powerful when building your page based on data received dynamically (for example, from a database or an XML document).

How do I do that?

To see these panels at work, create a new Windows application and name it DynamicLayout. Widen the form to a width of about 650, and drag a FlowLayoutPanel control onto the form, resizing it to fit.

You'll write code in the form's On_Load method to populate the panel dynamically. You can determine how controls will be added to the panel by setting the FlowDirection property of the panel, either in the properties box or dynamically (at runtime), to one of the four enumerated values (BottomUp, LeftToRight, RightToLeft, or TopDown). The default is LeftToRight.

In a truly data-driven application, you'd read a data source and decide what type of control to add, as well as what properties to set on that control. To keep the example simple, just add a fixed number of label controls:

```csharp
private void Form1_Load(object sender, EventArgs e)
{
    for (int i = 0; i < 15; i++)
    {
        Label myLabel = new Label( );
        myLabel.Text = "Dynamically generated label " + i;
        myLabel.Width = 200;
        flowLayoutPanel1.FlowDirection = FlowDirection.LeftToRight;
        flowLayoutPanel1.Controls.Add(myLabel);
    }
}
```

The FlowLayoutPanel control will add your controls based on the FlowDirection property you've set, as shown in Figure 3-21.

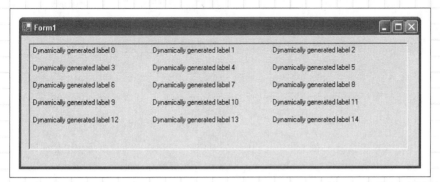

I set the BorderStyle property for the panel to Fixed3D to make the panel easier to see.

Figure 3-21. The flow layout panel

Notice that each label has been added to the form in the order specified by the FlowDirection property (left to right) and that all the controls are nicely aligned automatically.

TableLayoutPanel works similarly, except that this control gives you precise control over the size of its rows and columns, much as you'd expect from a table. To see this at work, remove the FlowLayoutPanel control from your form and replace it with a TableLayoutPanel control. The default setting is a panel with two rows and two columns, but you can set the ColumnCount property to any number you want—for this example, set it to 4. Set CellBorderStyle to Single so that we can see the cells, and set BackColor to a light blue so that the panel stands out.

You can adjust the size of each column or row by clicking the Edit Rows and Columns link, This opens the Column and Row Styles dialog box, as shown in Figure 3-22.

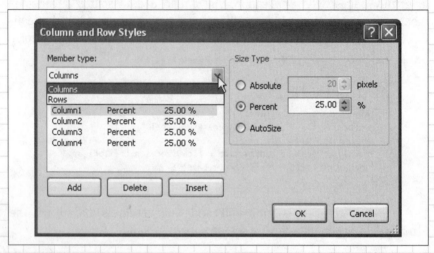

Figure 3-22. Editing columns and rows

Now you are ready to add controls to the table, on the fly:

```
for (int i = 0; i < 15; i++)
{
    Label myLabel = new Label();
    myLabel.Text = "Dynamically generated label " + i;
    myLabel.Width = 200;
    tableLayoutPanel1.Controls.Add(myLabel);
}
```

Notice that other than a change in the name of the panel, this code is identical to the code you used to add controls to the FlowLayoutPanel control.

What about...

...setting a property on an individual control within the panel?

You can access the controls on a form using the Find method. To do so, first make sure you add code to set the name of each control:

```
myLabel.Name = "Label" + i;
```

Now you can access an individual label (or a set of labels) using code similar to this:

```
Control[] foundControls = flowLayoutPanel1.Controls.Find("Label3", false);
Label theControl = (Label)foundControls[0];
theControl.Text = "Who is John Galt?";
```

The result is shown in Figure 3-23. (I circled the affected label.)

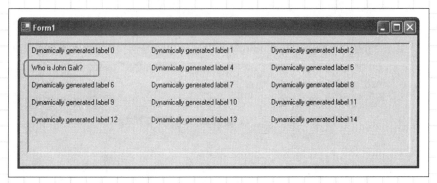

Figure 3-23. Editing a control within a panel

Where can I learn more?

Check the MSDN Help for information on the FlowLayoutPanel class and the TableLayoutPanel class.

Create Safe Asynchronous Tasks

.NET provides extensive support for multithreaded applications without requiring you to manage the threads. In .NET 2.0 the support for safe asynchronous tasks is greatly enhanced with the addition of the BackgroundWorker object, which allows you to work safely in a second thread while maintaining user interface control (for updates and cancellation) in your main thread. There is no need to spawn threads explicitly or to manage resource locking.

How do I do that?

To demonstrate how this works, you'll create a small Windows application that provides a reminder after a specified number of seconds have passed, as shown in Figure 3-24.

Figure 3-24. The Reminder application

You'll write the program so that when you click Start, the Start button and text boxes are disabled, and the Cancel button is enabled. While the timer is ticking down, a progress bar will show what percentage of time has expired, as shown in Figure 3-25.

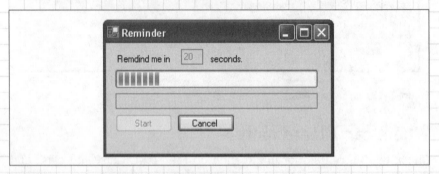

Figure 3-25. The Reminder application in progress

If you click Cancel, a cancel message is displayed. When the time has elapsed (or the timer is cancelled), the text is displayed, cancel is disabled, and the Start button and text boxes are enabled.

Be sure to set a reasonable default value in the txtSeconds control so that the user can click Start without throwing an exception.

To make this work, you want to have two different threads: one for the user interface and one for the timer. Create a new project and name it BackgroundWorkerDemo. Drag a BackgroundWorker object (from the Components tab in the Toolbox) onto the form (it appears in the component tray at the bottom).

Set the WorkerReportsProgress and WorkerSupportsCancellation properties to True so that you will receive both Progress and Cancellation events. Next, click the Events button in the properties window (the one with the lightening bolt on it) to see the three events supported by the BackgroundWorker object. Double-click each event to have Visual Studio

2005 set up the event handlers, which will be named backgroundWorker1_DoWork, backgroundWorker1_ProgressChanged, and backgroundWorker1_RunWorkerCompleted.

You are ready to create your timer within the BackgroundWorker object's thread, as shown in Example 3-1.

Example 3-1. Using the BackgroundWorker object

```
using System;
using System.Collections.Generic;
using System.ComponentModel;
using System.Data;
using System.Drawing;
using System.Threading;
using System.Windows.Forms;


namespace BackgroundWorkerDemo
{

    partial class Form1 : Form
    {

        public class TimerInfo
        {
            public string reminderMessage;
            public double numSeconds;
            public TimerInfo(string msg, double secs)
            {
                this.reminderMessage = msg;
                this.numSeconds = secs;
            }
        }


        public Form1()
        {
            InitializeComponent();
        }

        private void btnStart_Click(object sender, EventArgs e)
        {
            TimerInfo info =
                new TimerInfo(txtMessage.Text, Convert.ToDouble(this.txtSeconds.
Text));

            txtMessage.Text = string.Empty;
            SetEnabled(true);
            backgroundWorker1.RunWorkerAsync(info);
        }
```

Example 3-1. Using the BackgroundWorker object (continued)

```
private void SetEnabled(bool isRunning)
{
    this.btnStart.Enabled = !isRunning;
    this.btnCancel.Enabled = isRunning;
    this.txtSeconds.Enabled = !isRunning;
    this.txtMessage.Enabled = !isRunning;
    if (isRunning)
    {
        this.progressBar1.Value = 0;
    }
}

private void backgroundWorker1_DoWork(object sender, DoWorkEventArgs e)
{
    // This method will run on a thread other than the UI thread.
    // Be sure not to manipulate any Windows Forms controls created
    // on the UI thread from this method.
    BackgroundWorker worker = sender as BackgroundWorker;
    TimerInfo ti = (TimerInfo)e.Argument;

    DateTime startTime = DateTime.Now;
    do
    {
        if (worker.CancellationPending)
        {
            e.Cancel = true;
            return;
        }

        System.TimeSpan duration = DateTime.Now.Subtract(startTime);
        // chop down total seconds to an int
        double totalSeconds = duration.TotalSeconds;
        double percent = totalSeconds / ti.numSeconds * 100.0;
        int progressPercent = (int)percent;
        progressPercent = progressPercent > 100 ? 100 : progressPercent;
        worker.ReportProgress(progressPercent);
        Thread.Sleep(20);
    } while (DateTime.Now < startTime.AddSeconds(ti.numSeconds));

    // e.Result is available to the
    // RunWorkerCompleted event handler.
    e.Result = ti.reminderMessage;
}

//Update the progress bar
private void backgroundWorker1_ProgressChanged(
    object sender, ProgressChangedEventArgs e)
{
    this.progressBar1.Value = e.ProgressPercentage;
}

// handle work completed (update the ui)
```

Example 3-1. Using the BackgroundWorker object (continued)

```
private void backgroundWorker1_RunWorkerCompleted(
    object sender, RunWorkerCompletedEventArgs e)
{
    // Handle the case where an exception was thrown.
    if (e.Error != null)
    {
        MessageBox.Show(e.Error.Message);
    }
    else if (e.Cancelled)
    {
        txtMessage.Text = "CANCELLED. ";
        SetEnabled(false);
    }
    else
    {
        // the operation succeeded.
        txtMessage.Text = e.Result.ToString();
        SetEnabled(false);
    }
}

// cancel the thread and post cancellation message
private void btnCancel_Click(object sender, EventArgs e)
{
    this.backgroundWorker1.CancelAsync();
    SetEnabled(false);

}

    }
}
```

When the user clicks Start, the btnStart_Click event handler creates an instance of TimerInfo, a simple class I created to encapsulate the user's message and the number of seconds to count down. Then the Click event handler blanks out the message window, calls SetEnabled to disable the Start button and the text boxes, and calls the RunWorkerAsync method on the BackgroundWorker object, passing in the TimerInfo object as an argument.

Your call to RunWorkerAsync raises the DoWork event, which will be handled by your backgroundWorker1_DoWork event handler. That handler receives two arguments. The first is the instance of BackgroundWorker that you created, backgroundWorker1, and the second is an instance of DoWorkEventArgs.

The DoWorkEventArgs object has two useful properties: Argument, which is the TimerInfo object you passed in when you called RunWorkerAsync, and Result, which is how you pass results to the RunWorkerCompleted event handler.

The argument you pass to RunWorkerAsync will be available in the DoWork method as e.Argument. The method is overloaded to allow you to call RunWorkerAsync without passing in an argument, if none is needed.

Inside your event handler, backgroundWorker1_DoWork, you retrieve the BackgroundWorker object and the TimerInfo object:

```
BackgroundWorker worker = sender as BackgroundWorker;
TimerInfo ti = (TimerInfo)e.Argument;
```

Then you begin a loop that will continue until the time has expired:

```
do
{
    //…
}while (DateTime.Now < startTime.AddSeconds(ti.numSeconds));
```

Each time through the loop you check to see if the user has clicked Cancel. If not, you compute the percentage of time elapsed, and you call ReportProgress on BackgroundWorker, which fires the ProgressChanged event (which is handled by your backgroundWorker1_ProgressChanged event handler). Then you sleep 20 milliseconds, and start over.

The ProgressChanged event handler updates the progress bar based on the progress percentage, which is passed in as a property of ProgressChangedEventArgs.

Exiting DoWork automatically fires the RunWorkerCompleted event.

When the time expires, you set the Result property to the reminder message and exit DoWork:

```
e.Result = ti.reminderMessage;
```

Exiting DoWork automatically fires the RunWorkerCompleted event, which is handled by your backgroundWorker1_RunWorkerCompleted event handler.

In the backgroundWorker1_RunWorkerCompleted event handler, first check to see if an exception was thrown (in which case e.Error will be non-null):

```
if (e.Error != null)
{
    MessageBox.Show(e.Error.Message);
}
```

Then you check to see if you got to this handler because the work was cancelled (in which case e.Cancelled will be true):

```
else if (e.Cancelled)
{
    txtMessage.Text = "CANCELLED. ";
    SetEnabled(false);
}
```

Finally, if neither of those tests passes, you got here because the work is done and you can set the text of the message box to the value you reclaim from e.Result:

```
else
{
    txtMessage.Text = e.Result.ToString();
}
```

What about...

...using `BackgroundWorker` for other lengthy processes, such as downloading a file or data over the Internet?

This is an excellent solution for types that don't already provide asynchronous functionality (for example, overlapped I/O).

Where can I learn more?

`BackgroundWorker` is a very hot item in .NET 2.0, and a number of good articles are available on this subject on the Internet, including an excellent blog entry by Roy Osherove at *http://weblogs.asp.net/rosherove/archive/2004/06/16/156948.aspx*. Also, the MSDN includes an extensive write-up on `BackgroundWorker`.

Put the Web in a Window

.NET 2.0 provides a `WebBrowser` control that you can drag and drop directly into a Windows application. This gives you a full-featured Internet Explorer 6 browser embedded in your application, with virtually no coding required.

How do I do that?

Create a new Windows application (`WebBrowsing`) and enlarge the form to hold a reasonably sized browser and a couple of other controls. Drag a `WebBrowser` control onto your form. You'll notice that it fills the form, but if you use its smart tag to click Undock in the parent container, you'll find you have a resizable `WebBrowser` control within the form.

Click the `URL` property of the `WebBrowser` control and type the URL of your favorite web site (for example, *http://www.LibertyAssociates.com*). Run the application and voila! You're browsing my site.

Let's add a few useful controls: a text box (with auto-complete for URLs), a progress bar, and Back and Forward buttons.

The browser control fires a number of useful events as the page is loading. Some of the most useful are shown in Table 3-6.

You can drag a full featured Internet Explorer 6 browser directly into your Windows application.

Notice that loading the page is accomplished asynchronously— for example, your application keeps running while the page is loading.

Table 3-6. Browser events

Browser event	Description
Navigating	Raised when you set a new URL, or when the user clicks a link. (Use this to cancel navigation.)
Navigated	Raised just before the web browser begins downloading the page.
ProgressChanged	Raised periodically during a download. Tells you how many bytes have been downloaded and how many are expected. (Use this to create a progress bar.)
DocumentCompleted	Raised when the page is fully loaded.

Double-click each button on your form to set up their event handlers. Click the browser itself, and set a handler for the ProgressChanged event. Finally, set the Leave event for the browser, and set two events for the URL text box. The complete source code listing is shown in Example 3-2.

Example 3-2. Integrating the WebBrowser control into your form

```
using System;
using System.Collections.Generic;
using System.ComponentModel;
using System.Data;
using System.Drawing;
using System.Text;
using System.Windows.Forms;

namespace WebBrowsing
{
    public partial class Form1 : Form
    {
        public Form1()
        {
            InitializeComponent();
        }
        private void webBrowser1_ProgressChanged(
            object sender, WebBrowserProgressChangedEventArgs e)
        {
            progressBar1.Value = (int)(e.CurrentProgress / e.MaximumProgress);
        }

        private void btnBack_Click(object sender, EventArgs e)
        {
            webBrowser1.GoBack();
        }

        private void btnForward_Click(object sender, EventArgs e)
        {
            webBrowser1.GoForward();
        }
```

```
    private void btnStop_Click(object sender, EventArgs e)
    {
        webBrowser1.Stop();
    }

    private void txtURL_Leave(object sender, EventArgs e)
    {
        if (txtURL.Text.Length < 1)
        {
            txtURL.Text = "http://www.LibertyAssociates.com";
        }

        webBrowser1.Url = txtURL.Text;

    }

    private void webBrowser1_DocumentCompleted(
        object sender, WebBrowserDocumentCompletedEventArgs e)
    {
        txtURL.Text = webBrowser1.Url.ToString();
    }
  }
}
```

The only tricky code is for computing the value for the progress bar (which must be cast to an int).

The result is shown in Figure 3-26.

What about...

...using the WebBrowser control to launch a standalone browser?

You can do this; instead of setting the URL property just use the over-loaded Navigate method:

```
    public void Navigate(
        string url,
        bool newWindow  // set true for new window
    );
```

...what about using the WebBrowser control to look at XML files with full collapse/expand support?

Sure; just navigate to the XML file and the WebBrowser control will do the work for you, as illustrated in Figure 3-27.

The WebBrowser control provides methods that duplicate the browser functions every web surfer is familiar with, such as Stop, Refresh, GoBack, GoForward, GoHome, GoSearch, Print, ShowPrintDialog, and ShowSaveAsDialog.

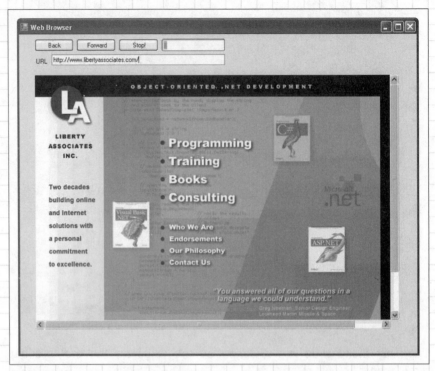

Figure 3-26. Browsing the Web

Where can I learn more?

The .NET Framework Windows Forms page (*http://www.windowsforms.net/*) covers this feature, as does the "WebBrowser Control" article in the MSDN.

Enable One-Click Deployment

ClickOnce lets you distribute rich client applications over standard web protocols.

Many would argue that web applications have a huge advantage over Windows applications in that they can be distributed so easily (at so little cost). Some developers and clients have been frustrated, however, that the browser limits their control over the user interface, and thus the idea of a *smart client* (sometimes called a rich client, but not to be confused with the thick clients of the client-server era) was born.

A smart client is a Windows-based application that you can deploy by asking your users to click a link presented in their browser. A smart client uses the power of Windows on a desktop Windows machine to provide a richer user experience than is possible with a web browser, and in this regard it resembles a traditional Windows application. But unlike a

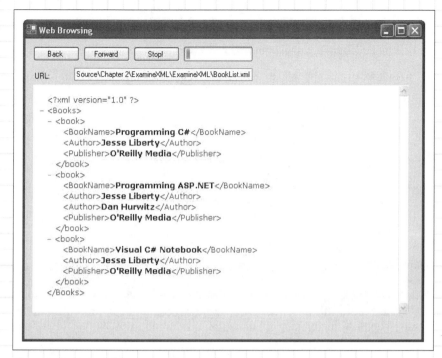

Figure 3-27. Examining an XML file

Windows app, a smart client is distributed to users via the Web (holding down distribution costs) and uses centralized data (and possibly some processing) via one or more web services. A smart client application is essentially a web application that is viewed through a rich client-side application and is distributed and updated using web protocols.

How do I do that?

The key to creating a smart client is a new technology called *click-once deployment*, dubbed ClickOnce by Microsoft. ClickOnce allows your customer to download your application to a local machine. When you update your application on your server, the client is notified and is offered an opportunity to update.

To see this cool new feature at work, create a new Windows application project and call it ClickOnce. Drag a label and a button control onto the application form. Double-click the button and add this line of code:

```
label1.Text = "Hi.";
```

Run your application to make sure it works. This simplistic application will stand in for the rich client you would normally create.

To make this a ClickOnce client you'll need to have Internet Information Server (IIS) installed.

Your next step is to build the application for ClickOnce distribution by choosing Build → Publish ClickOnce, as shown in Figure 3-28.

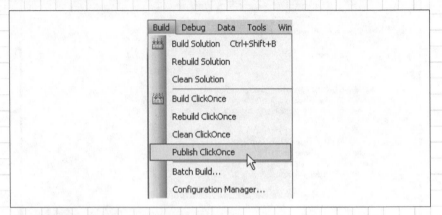

Figure 3-28. Publishing your ClickOnce application

This menu choice brings up the Publish Wizard, where you can indicate the virtual path from which your application will be distributed, as shown in Figure 3-29.

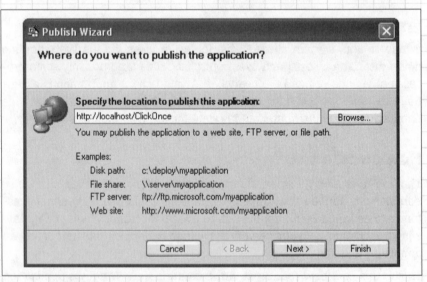

Figure 3-29. Specifying the ClickOnce location

Once you set the virtual path, the second step of the wizard asks if you want to make the application available online or offline, or only for use online. Typically users choose to make the application available online or offline (see Figure 3-30).

Figure 3-30. Choosing availability

The third and final step is to create a strong name for your application. You have a choice at this point to either have the wizard generate a strong name for you or use a key provider that you have already established.

When you click Next, the wizard reviews your choices and informs you that when the application is installed on the client machine, a shortcut will be added to the Start menu, and that your application can be uninstalled from the client machine using the Add/Remove programs.

Then the wizard opens a browser and navigates to the default download page for your application, as shown in Figure 3-31.

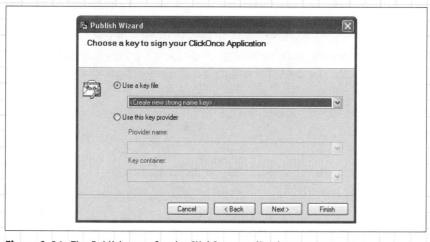

Figure 3-31. The Publish page for the ClickOnce application

If you click Install ClickOnce and install the application, you'll find that it is now listed in your start menu, as shown in Figure 3-32.

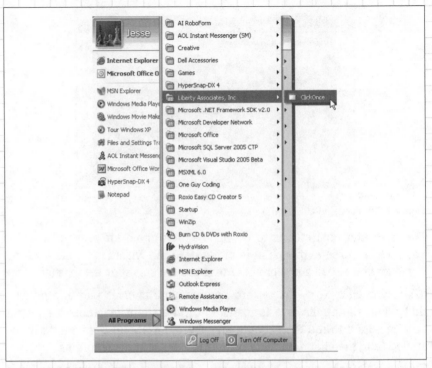

Figure 3-32. The application installed on the Start menu

What about...

...when you update a ClickOnce application on your server?

ClickOnce makes the update available the next time the user tries to use the application if the user is connected to the server (via the Internet or a local area network).

To see this at work, return to the application and change the Click handler:

```
label1.Text = "Updated.";
```

Repeat the previous steps using the Publish Wizard.

TIP

When you get to the set for the key, use the key already assigned to the application (this will be the default). This indicates that the newly built application is a replacement, not a new program.

The next time the user runs your application, the Update Available dialog will be presented, as shown in Figure 3-33.

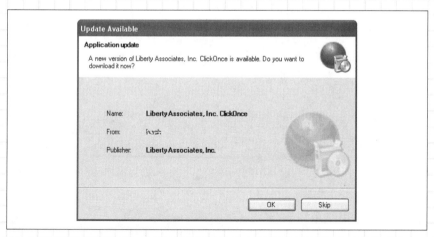

Figure 3-33. The Update Available dialog

Click OK. Your program is updated and when you run it you will see the new behavior.

Where can I learn more?

O'Reilly's ONDotnet.com site has a good article on ClickOnce at *http://www.ondotnet.com/pub/a/dotnet/2004/10/11/clickonce.html*. Also check out "Deploy and Update Your Smart Client Projects Using a Central Server," by Brian Noyes, in *MSDN Magazine* (*http://msdn.microsoft.com/msdnmag/issues/04/05/ClickOnce/*).

CHAPTER 4

Web Applications

The ASP.NET team at Microsoft set an ambitious goal for ASP.NET 2.0: to make it possible for web-site developers to build ASP.NET applications with 75% less coding. Their success means you will write *a lot* less plumbing code when you build ASP.NET 2.0-based applications, so that instead you can focus on making your web applications accessible and secure for your customers and clients. Among the improvements you'll find in ASP.NET 2.0 are powerful new controls, including data access controls that free you from repetitive database programming, and security controls that enable you to better manage user accounts and passwords. Also available are new controls for managing access to site data and for offering a uniform user experience across your web site's pages.

All of these features are available to C# programmers in all editions of Visual Studio 2005, with the exception of Visual C# 2005 Express Edition. Best of all, you no longer need Internet Information Server (IIS) to develop an ASP.NET application, a feature we'll investigate in the first lab.

Develop Web Apps Without IIS

With Visual Studio 2005 you no longer need to install and use IIS to host your web applications while you develop them. Now Visual Studio gives you four choices:

File System Web Site
 This is the simplest alternative; just put all your files in a filesystem folder on your hard drive.

Local IIS Web Site

This works just like it did with ASP.NET 1.x. You can use Visual Studio 2005 to create web applications that reside either on the local IIS root or in a virtual directory.

Remote Web Site

You can use Visual Studio 2005 to create applications that reside on remote servers as long as those servers support FrontPage 2000 Server Extensions.

FTP Web Site

Visual Studio 2005 allows you to create and maintain web sites on an FTP server.

How do I do that?

The first option, a filesystem-based web site, not only is completely new with ASP.NET 2.0, but also is one of the easiest ways to create a web application. You're likely to use it often. Let's explore that option here. To get started, open Visual Studio 2005 and choose File → New → Web Site..., as shown in Figure 4-1.

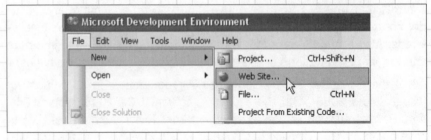

Figure 4-1. Creating a new web site in Visual Studio 2005

This menu choice opens the New Web Site dialog shown in Figure 4-2. Select ASP.NET Web Site in the Templates pane of the dialog. In the Location box choose File System. In the Language box choose Visual C# (this is, after all, a book on C#). Then in the box to the right of the Location box, choose a folder to house your ASP.NET files.

Click OK. You are placed into the *Default.aspx* file, in Source view. Select Design view instead.

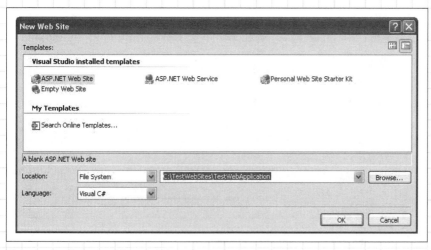

Figure 4-2. The New Web Site dialog

TIP

Note two changes from Visual Studio 2003. Now the default is to put you in Source view rather than Design view, and within Design view the default is a flow layout rather than a grid layout. Thus, if you want absolute positioning, you must switch to grid layout. For this book we will follow the tradition of most web programmers and use tables for laying out pages when specific placement is needed.

Drag a label control and a button control from the Toolbox onto the form and double-click the button to open the code-behind file for the page. Notice (as noted in Chapter 1) that Visual Studio 2005 web forms use partial classes by default, so all the supporting code is not made visible to you.

In the Button1_Click event handler, enter this code:

```
Label1.Text = "Hello.";
```

Try to run the application in debug mode. Visual Studio 2005 will interrupt to point out that you need a *Web.config* file with debugging enabled, as shown in Figure 4-3.

The default choice is to allow Visual Studio 2005 to create a *Web.config* file for you. Click OK.

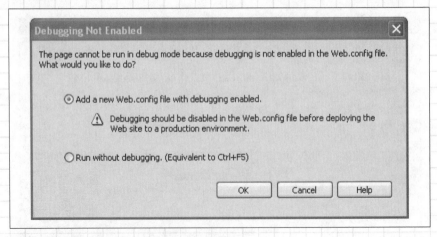

Figure 4-3. The Debugging Not Enabled dialog

What just happened?

You'll notice that a lot of things happened at once. You'll see a notification in your taskbar that Visual Studio 2005 has started the Visual Web Developer Web Server, as shown in Figure 4-4.

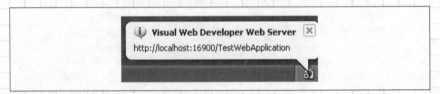

Figure 4-4. Visual Web Developer Web Server started

TIP

Visual Studio 2005 starts an instance of Visual Web Developer Web Server to test your application. Unlike IIS, which includes a web server, FTP server, SMTP server, and other facilities, the Visual Web Developer Web Server is used only to test web applications during their development.

Clicking your web form button will cause a post back to the Visual Web Developer Web Server and an update of the button label, just as if this application were being served by IIS. A quick look at the Solution Explorer will also confirm that Visual Studio has added the *Web.config* file to your project files.

What about...

...editing the *Web.config* file that Visual Studio creates for me? Can I do that?

You can edit the file by hand, but it is much easier to edit it using the new Web Site Administration Tool (WAT).

Access the WAT by opening a browser and navigating directly to your *.axd* file (for example, *http://localhost/TestWebApplication/Webadmin.axd*) or, more easily, from Visual Studio 2005. To open the WAT from within Visual Studio 2005 choose Website → ASP.NET Configuration. The WAT for your application will open in a browser with four tabs, as shown in Figure 4-5.

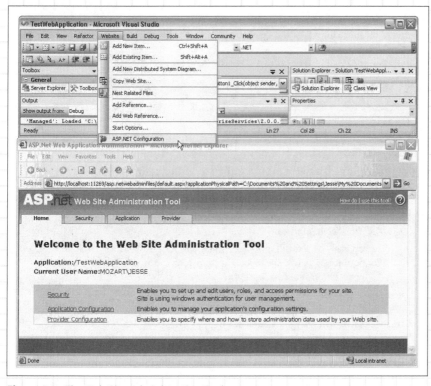

Figure 4-5. The Web Site Administration Tool page

Click the Application tab for links to pages that will allow you to create *Web.config* settings painlessly and accurately, as shown in Figure 4-6.

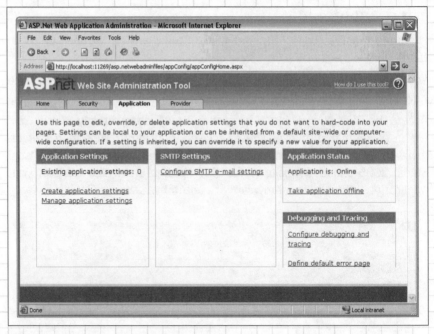

Figure 4-6. Configuring web settings

TIP

The Web Site Administration Tool page shown in Figure 4-5 is actually an ASP.NET application. You'll find the source code on your hard drive at *c:\[WindowsDirectory]\Microsoft.NET\Framework\[Version]\ ASP.NETWebAdminFiles*.

Look closely at the URL displayed when you choose Website → ASP.NET Configuration. It will show you exactly which file it is displaying (e.g., *[…]/appConfig/DebugandTrace.aspx*).

...what about deploying a file-based system?

Just copy the contents of your folder to a virtual folder on the server, and you're all set.

Where can I learn more?

The Web Site Administration Tool is reviewed in great detail in the MSDN Help files under the article "Web Site Administration Tool Overview." Also, if you do a Google search for "ASP.NET Web Site Administration Tool" you will get literally thousands of hits, many of which will lead to articles on how to get the most out of this useful utility.

Provide Forms-Based Security Without Code

One of the most common tasks in building a publicly available web application is to create forms-based security, in which you allow your users to log in with a password (rather than, for example, not logging in, or using Windows-based authentication).

To make forms-based security work, you need to authenticate your users. In ASP.NET 2.0, adding this feature is greatly simplified by new controls that handle most of the plumbing for you.

Now creating forms-based security, complete with login screens and password maintenance, is provided in a set of related ASP.NET controls.

How do I do that?

To explore new support for forms-based security in ASP.NET 2.0, let's build a simple application. In this lab, you'll work through the following steps:

1. Set up the application database.
2. Create the application folder as a virtual directory, setting its security type to Forms.
3. Create a web site.
4. Add login controls.
5. Verify that the user database is updated.
6. Create a Welcome page.
7. Create the Login page.

Set up the application database

ASP.NET 2.0 forms-based security is based on a set of tables that must be created in your database, typically SQL Server or SQL Server Express. Fortunately, ASP.NET provides a utility named *aspnet_regsql.exe*, located in the *[Drive:]\Windows\Microsoft.NET\Framework\[versionNumber]* folder on your web server, which sets up the tables for you. This utility program will create the required database and all its tables.

The easiest way to use this utility is to run the *aspnet_regsql.exe* utility from the .NET command box, with no arguments. A wizard will be started that will walk you through the process. For more details, see the MSDN article "Installing the SQL Server Provider Database."

Create a folder as a virtual directory; set its security to Forms

Start by creating an empty directory on your local drive. Call it *FormsBasedSecurity*. Open the IIS Manager and create a virtual directory to point to your new directory.

TIP

To open IIS Manager from the Windows Start menu select Control Panel → Administrative Tools → Internet Information Server.

To create a virtual directory, click the server name (typically your local computer) and then click Web Sites. Right-click Default Web Site, choose New → Virtual Directory, and work your way through the wizard, just as you did in ASP.NET 1.x.

After you've created the virtual directory, right-click it within the IIS Administrator and choose Properties. Click the ASP.NET tab of the properties window, and then click Edit Configuration to open the ASP.NET Configuration Settings dialog.

Within the ASP.NET Configuration Settings dialog click the Authentication tab, and within that tab set the "Authentication mode" to Forms and the "Membership provider class" to AspNetSqlMembershipProvider, as shown in Figure 4-7.

Click the General tab, and if LocalSqlServer is not set to the database you use, set the connection parameters so that the data source is set to your database (for example, *sqlexpress*), as shown in Figure 4-8.

Click OK to close the dialogs and return to the directory you created, where you'll find a *Web.config* file containing the following XML:

```xml
<?xml version="1.0" encoding="utf-8"?>
<configuration>
   <connectionStrings>
   <remove name="LocalSqlServer" />
   <add name="LocalSqlServer" connectionString="data source=.\
sqlexpress;Integrated Security=SSPI;Initial Catalog=aspnetdb" />
   </connectionStrings>
   <system.web>
       <authentication mode="Forms" />
       <membership defaultProvider="AspNetSqlMembershipProvider" />
   </system.web>
</configuration>
```

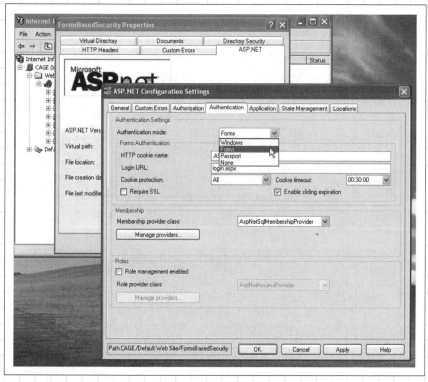

Figure 4-7. Setting forms authentication

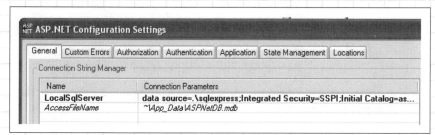

Figure 4-8. Setting the connection parameters

Create the new web site

Open Visual Studio 2005 and create a new web site in the same directory. Visual Studio will interrupt and tell you that the site already exists, as shown in Figure 4-9.

Select "Open the existing Web site" and your application should open with its *Web.config* file in place.

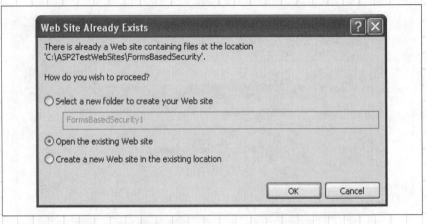

Figure 4-9. Opening the existing web site

In this test application you will create three pages:

Welcome

The Welcome page will display different information depending on whether the user has logged in.

Login

The Login page presents a form where members can enter a username and a password.

AddUser

For users to log in, first you must create a database of users to keep track of user accounts. This requires you to add a page to your site that lets users sign up for accounts in the first place.

Begin by creating the AddUser web page and calling it *AddUser.aspx*, as shown in Figure 4-10.

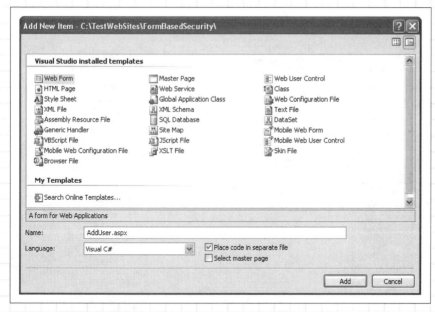

Figure 4-10. Creating a new .aspx page

TIP

Selecting "Place code in separate file" causes Visual Studio to use the code-behind model, instead of placing the code in a script block in the same file as the one containing the web controls.

Add login controls

Click the Design tab for your *.aspx* page, and then click the Login tab in the Visual Studio Toolbox. Drag an instance of `CreateUserWizard` onto your page, as shown in Figure 4-11.

The `CreateUserWizard` control will prompt the user for a username, a password (twice), an email address, and a security question and answer. All of this is configurable through the HTML that is created by this control.

Click the control and scroll through the properties to find the `ContinueDestinationPageURL` property. Click the Browse button and choose the *AddUser.aspx* page so that you'll be brought back to the same page after the new user is confirmed.

Finally, set the *AddUser.aspx* page as your Start page, and then test the application. After being prompted to update *Web.config* to allow debugging, you'll be brought to the Create User Wizard. Fill in the form, as shown in Figure 4-12.

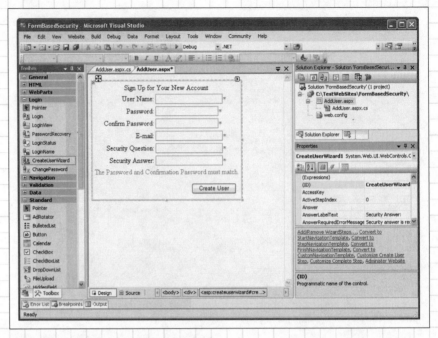

Figure 4-11. The CreateUserWizard control

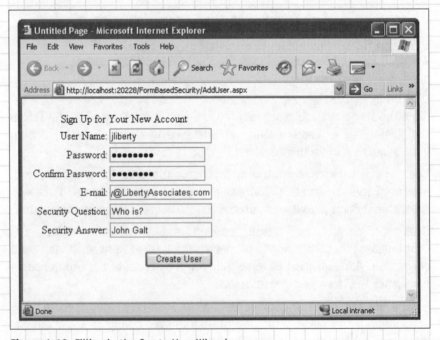

Figure 4-12. Filling in the Create User Wizard

Click the Create User button. You should see a confirmation screen and a button marked Continue. Clicking Continue will bring you back to the Create Account form where you can add another user. Add a few users and test the built-in validation the wizard provides; you'll find that you can't enter the same username twice, that the two passwords must match, and that the required fields must have text. All of this is managed by FieldValidator controls within the HTML created by the Wizard control.

Verify that the user database is updated

Stop your project and look at the Database Explorer, where you will find the tables within the *aspnetdb* database you created earlier, as shown in Figure 4-13.

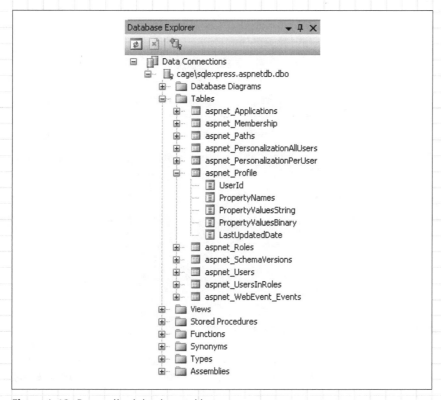

Figure 4-13. Personalized database tables

Create the Welcome page

With your user database in place you are ready to create the Welcome page that will welcome the logged-in user.

Create a new page called *Default.aspx* and drag a `LoginStatus` control from the Login section of the Toolbox.

A link marked Login is placed on the page whose smart tag indicates that you are looking at the template you would see when no user is logged in, as shown in Figure 4–14.

Figure 4-14. Not-logged-in view

You can set the properties of the `LoginStatus` control to, for example, change the text of the link. You can also drop down the view window to see the link and text for logged-in status.

Drag a `LoginView` control from the Toolbox and drop it onto the page below the `LoginStatus` control. Here you can enter text and controls that will be displayed based on whether the user is logged in. Notice that this control has two views: AnonymousTemplate and LoggedInTemplate. Which template is displayed depends on whether the user has logged in.

Click the smart tag, confirm that the view is set to AnonymousTemplate, and type some text in the box, as shown in Figure 4–15.

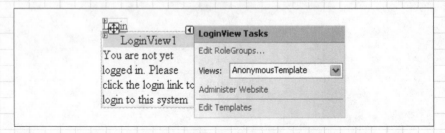

Figure 4-15. AnonymousTemplate view

Now change the view on `LoginView` to LoggedInTemplate. Drag a `LoginName` control onto the template so that you can welcome the user by name, as shown in Figure 4–16.

Create the Login page

You are finally ready to create the Login page. Add a new page named *Login.aspx*. Change to Design view, and drag a `Login` control onto the page. Just for fun, click the Auto Format link from the smart tag, as shown in Figure 4–17.

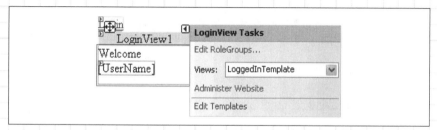

Figure 4-16. Using UserName to welcome the user

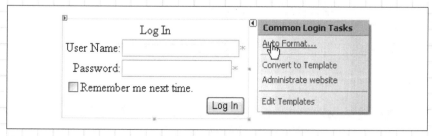

Figure 4-17. Creating the Login control

Choose a look you like for the Login control.

You're all set. Make sure the *Default.aspx* page is the Start page, and run the application. The default page will inform you that you are not logged in and will offer a link to the Login page.

When you go to the Login page, enter a false login name and/or an incorrect password. The Login control informs you of the mistake, as shown in Figure 4-18.

Enter the correct name and password, and you are brought back to the Welcome page. Your status as logged in is noted, you are greeted by name, and you are offered the opportunity to log out.

You've created an entire login architecture without writing a line of code.

What about...

...if users forget their passwords?

The new PasswordRecovery control gives users a way to recover. Drag onto the form a PasswordRecovery control from the Login tab in the Toolbox (or create a link to a new page with this control). The user will be prompted first for a known username, and then with the question and answer you created earlier when you were creating a user, as shown in Figure 4-19. If they match, the password will be sent by email.

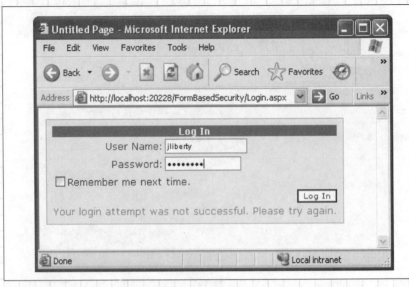

Figure 4-18. An incorrect login, caught

Identity Confirmation
Answer the following question to receive your password.
User Name: jliberty
Question: Who is?
Answer: [   ]

Submit

Figure 4-19. Confirming the user's identity

...what if I want users to change their passwords?

Add a ChangePassword control to your page (for example, to *Default.aspx*). The user will be prompted for the original password and then for the new password, as shown in Figure 4-20.

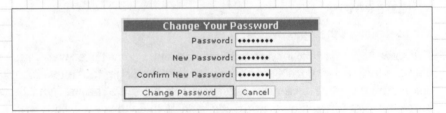

Figure 4-20. Changing the user's password

If all three fields are correct, the password will change in the database.

Where can I learn more?

For more information, see my article on forms-based security, titled "ASP.NET Forms" and available on O'Reilly's ONDotnet.com site at *http://www.ondotnet.com*. In addition, an excellent article in the June 2004 issue of *MSDN Magazine*, titled "Security Headaches? Take ASP.NET 2.0" and written by Keith Brown, is available online. Finally, you might want to read the article "ASP.NET Web Site Security" in the MSDN Library.

Add Roles to ASP.NET Accounts

You can assign a set of permissions to a group of people. You do so in two steps: first you assign permissions to a role, and then you assign users to the roles you've created. Any given user can be in more than one role (e.g., administrator and manager). The permissions you assign to each role can determine access to a page or can determine the content of a given page displayed to members of that role.

Roles are named groups of permissions to which you can assign users.

How do I do that?

To demonstrate how to create roles and assign users to those roles, you'll need to create a new application, setting the appropriate IIS configuration. In the previous lab you created the directory for your application before you created the application itself. To see that you can create the relationship between physical and virtual directories in more than one way, this time let's reverse the order. Start by creating a new web application (called SecurityRoles).

Find the directory in which the *Default.aspx* page is held by clicking the page in the Solution Explorer and looking at the properties window. Use the IIS Administrator to create a virtual directory called *SecurityRoles* that points to that physical directory. Right-click the virtual directory and select Properties.

Click the ASP.NET tab and the Edit Configuration button (as you did in the previous lab). Once again click the Authentication tab and set Forms Authentication, but this time be sure to check the "Role management enabled" checkbox, as shown in Figure 4-21.

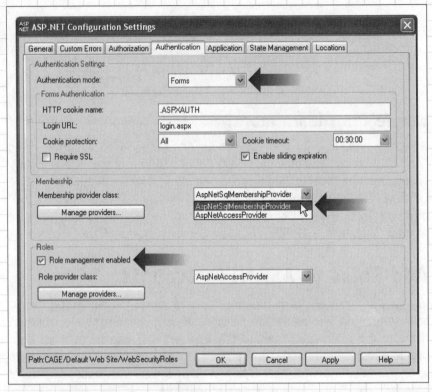

Figure 4-21. Checking role management

When you click OK and close the configuration dialogs, you'll find that a *Web.config* file has been added to the directory:

```
<?xml version="1.0"?>
<configuration>
   <connectionStrings>
   <remove name="LocalSqlServer" />
   <add name="LocalSqlServer" connectionString="data source=.\
sqlexpress;Integrated Security=SSPI;Initial Catalog=aspnetdb" />
   </connectionStrings>
   <system.web>
       <membership defaultProvider="AspNetSqlMembershipProvider" />
   <authentication mode="Forms"/>
       <roleManager enabled="True" defaultProvider="AspNetSqlRoleProvider" />
       <compilation debug="true"/></system.web>
</configuration>
```

Notice that this time, the roleManager element has been added and its enabled attribute has been set to true.

Now you need to add to this lab the pages from the previous lab.

One way to add these pages is to copy the *.aspx* and *.aspx.cs* files (that is
all the files except *Web.config*) to the new directory.

Once you've done this, return to Visual Studio 2005 and, in the Solution
Explorer, right-click the project and choose Add Existing Items to add the
pages from the earlier lab to this one. Now you are set to add roles to this
project.

Add two HyperLink controls to the default page. The first link should
contain the words *Add User* and the second link should contain the
words *Manage Roles*. The first link will redirect the user to the *AddUser*
page you imported (set NavigateUrl by clicking the ellipses and selecting the *CreateAccount.aspx* page). Go to *AddUser.aspx* and change the
ContinueDestinationPageURL property of the CreateUserWizard control
to the default page so that each time you add a user you will be brought
back to the *Default.aspx* page.

Create a new *ManageRoles.aspx* page. This page has a somewhat complex layout because it must display the list of roles and the list of users
supported by your site, as well as which users have been assigned which
roles. The complete *.aspx* listing is shown in Example 4-1, though it
might be easier to download this code from either the O'Reilly or Liberty
Associates web site.

Example 4-1. The ManageRoles.aspx page

```
<%@ Page Language="C#" AutoEventWireup="true"
CodeFile="ManageRoles.aspx.cs" Inherits="ManageRoles_aspx" %>

<!DOCTYPE html PUBLIC "-//W3C//DTD XHTML 1.1//EN" "http://www.w3.org/TR/xhtml11/
DTD/xhtml11.dtd">
<html xmlns="http://www.w3.org/1999/xhtml">
<head id="Head1" runat="server">
    <title>Manage Roles</title>
</head>
<body>
    <form id="form1" runat="server">
  <h3>Role Membership
      <asp:HyperLink ID="linkHome" Runat="server" NavigateUrl="~/Default.aspx">
Home page</asp:HyperLink>
  </h3>
  <asp:Label id="Msg" ForeColor="maroon" runat="server" /><BR>
  <table CellPadding="3" border="0">
    <tr>
      <td valign="top">Roles:</td>
      <td valign="top" style="width: 186px"><asp:ListBox id="RolesListBox"
          runat="server" Rows="8" AutoPostBack="True">
      </asp:ListBox></td>
      <td valign="top">Users:</td>
      <td valign="top"><asp:ListBox id="UsersListBox" DataTextField="Username"
        Rows="8" SelectionMode="Multiple" runat="server" /></td>
      <td valign="top" visible="false">
          <table>
          <tr>
              <td>
                  <asp:Button Text="Add User(s) to Role" id="btnAddUsersToRole"
                  runat="server" OnClick="AddUsers_OnClick" />
              </td>
          </tr>
          <tr>
              <td>
                  <asp:Button Text="Create new Role" id="btnCreateRole"
                  runat="server" OnClick="CreateRole_OnClick"
                  Width="170px" Height="24px" />
              </td>
          </tr>
          <tr>
          <td>
          <asp:Panel ID="pnlCreateRole" Runat="server" Width="259px"
          Height="79px" Visible="False" BackColor="#E0E0E0">
              <br />
                
              <asp:Label ID="Label2" Runat="server" Text="New Role:"
                Width="72px" Height="19px"/>
              <asp:TextBox ID="txtNewRole" Runat="server"/> <br />
                <br />
                         
                        
```

Example 4-1. The ManageRoles.aspx page (continued)

```
            <asp:Button ID="btnAddRole" Runat="server"
                Text="Add" OnClick="btnAddRole_Click"
                Width="64px" Height="24px" /><br />
        </asp:Panel>

        </td>
        </tr>
        </table>
    </td>
  </tr>
  <tr>
    <td valign="top">Users In Role:</td>
    <td valign="top" style="width: 186px">
        <asp:GridView runat="server" CellPadding="4" id="UsersInRoleGrid"
                            AutoGenerateColumns="false" Gridlines="None"
                            CellSpacing="0"
        OnRowCommand="UsersInRoleGrid_RemoveFromRole">
                    <HeaderStyle BackColor="navy" ForeColor="white" />
                    <Columns>
                      <asp:TemplateField HeaderText="User Name">
                        <ItemTemplate>
                          <%# Container.DataItem.ToString() %>
                        </ItemTemplate>
                      </asp:TemplateField>
                      <asp:ButtonField Text="Remove From Role"
ButtonType="Link" />
                    </Columns>
        </asp:GridView>
      </td>
    </tr>
  </table>
  </form>
</body>
</html>
```

TIP

This page is designed to be useful, not pretty. It is based on a demonstration *.aspx* page provided by Microsoft with beta software.

The complete code associated with the *ManageRoles.aspx* page is listed in Example 4-2.

Example 4-2. The complete ManageRoles.aspx code

```
using System;
using System.Data;
using System.Configuration;
using System.Collections;
```

Example 4-2. The complete ManageRoles.aspx code (continued)

```csharp
using System.Web;
using System.Web.Security;
using System.Web.UI;
using System.Web.UI.WebControls;
using System.Web.UI.WebControls.WebParts;
using System.Web.UI.HtmlControls;

public partial class ManageRoles_aspx : System.Web.UI.Page
{
    string[] rolesArray;
    MembershipUserCollection users;
    string[] usersInRole;

    public void Page_Load()
    {
        Msg.Text = "";

        if (!IsPostBack)
        {
            rolesArray = Roles.GetAllRoles();
            RolesListBox.DataSource = rolesArray;
            RolesListBox.DataBind();

            // Bind users to ListBox.

            users = Membership.GetAllUsers();
            UsersListBox.DataSource = users;
            UsersListBox.DataBind();
        }

        if (RolesListBox.SelectedItem != null)
        {
            // Show users in role. Bind user list to GridView.

            usersInRole = Roles.GetUsersInRole(RolesListBox.SelectedItem.Value);
            UsersInRoleGrid.DataSource = usersInRole;
            UsersInRoleGrid.DataBind();
        }
    }

    // void AddUsersButton_Click(object sender, EventArgs e)

    public void AddUsers_OnClick(object sender, EventArgs args)
    {
        // Verify that a role is selected.

        if (RolesListBox.SelectedItem == null)
        {
            Msg.Text = "Please select a role.";
            return;
        }
```

Example 4-2. The complete ManageRoles.aspx code (continued)

```
        // Verify that at least one user is selected.

        if (UsersListBox.SelectedItem == null)
        {
            Msg.Text = "Please select one or more users.";
            return;
        }

        // Create list of users to be added to the selected role.

        string[] newusers = new string[UsersListBox.GetSelectedIndices().Length];

        for (int i = 0; i < newusers.Length; i++)
        {
            newusers[i] =
                UsersListBox.Items[UsersListBox.GetSelectedIndices()[i]].Value;
        }


        // Add the users to the selected role.

        try
        {
            Roles.AddUsersToRole(newusers, RolesListBox.SelectedItem.Value);

            // Re-bind users in role to GridView.

            usersInRole = Roles.GetUsersInRole(RolesListBox.SelectedItem.Value);
            UsersInRoleGrid.DataSource = usersInRole;
            UsersInRoleGrid.DataBind();
        }
        catch (HttpException e)
        {
            Msg.Text = e.Message;
        }
    }


    public void UsersInRoleGrid_RemoveFromRole(object sender,
GridViewCommandEventArgs args)
    {
        // Get the selected username to remove.

        int index = Convert.ToInt32(args.CommandArgument);

        string username = ((DataBoundLiteralControl)UsersInRoleGrid.Rows[index].
Cells[0].Controls[0]).Text;


        // Remove the user from the selected role.
```

Example 4-2. The complete ManageRoles.aspx code (continued)

```
    try
    {
        Roles.RemoveUserFromRole(username, RolesListBox.SelectedItem.Value);
    }
    catch (Exception e)
    {
        Msg.Text = "An exception of type " + e.GetType().ToString() +
            " was encountered removing the user from the role.";
    }


    // Re-bind users in role to GridView.

    usersInRole = Roles.GetUsersInRole(RolesListBox.SelectedItem.Value);
    UsersInRoleGrid.DataSource = usersInRole;
    UsersInRoleGrid.DataBind();
}
public void CreateRole_OnClick(object sender, EventArgs e)
{
    pnlCreateRole.Visible = true;
}
/// <summary>
/// Handles clicking the Add button in the panel made
/// visible by clicking Create New Role
/// </summary>
public void btnAddRole_Click(object sender, EventArgs e)
{
    // make sure you have some text in the name of the role
    if (txtNewRole.Text.Length > 0)
    {
        string newRole = txtNewRole.Text;

        // if the role does not already exist, add it
        // rebind the RolesListBox to show the new role
        if (Roles.RoleExists(newRole) == false)
        {
            Roles.CreateRole(newRole);
            rolesArray = Roles.GetAllRoles();
            RolesListBox.DataSource = rolesArray;
            RolesListBox.DataBind();
        }
    }

    pnlCreateRole.Visible = false;
}
}
```

What just happened?

Here's how the code works. The logic begins with the Create Role button's onClick event handler, which makes the Create Role panel visible:

```
void CreateRole_OnClick(object sender, EventArgs e)
{
    pnlCreateRole.Visible = true;
}
```

The panel contains a text box (New Role) that you use to name a new role, and a button (Add) to add the new role to the roles collection, as shown in Figure 4-22.

Figure 4-22. The New Role panel

When you click the Add button, the btnAddRole_Click event handler is called:

```
void btnAddRole_Click(object sender, EventArgs e)
{
    if (txtNewRole.Text.Length > 0)
    {
        string newRole = txtNewRole.Text;

        if (Roles.RoleExists(newRole) == false)
        {
            Roles.CreateRole(newRole);
            rolesArray = Roles.GetAllRoles();
            RolesListBox.DataSource = rolesArray;
            RolesListBox.DataBind();
        }
    }
}
```

Assuming there is text in the New Role text box, you check whether the role already exists; if it doesn't you create a new role using the static CreateRole method of the Roles class provided by .NET 2.0.

Then you get all the roles and rebind the listbox, which now will include the new role, as shown in Figure 4-23.

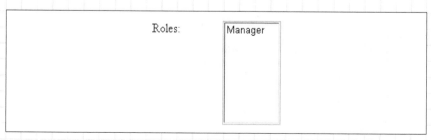

Figure 4-23. The Roles listbox

Once the new role is added, the panel is closed:

```
pnlCreateRole.Visible = false;
```

Run the application. If you are starting with a new database add some users. Next, click Add Roles and add a couple of roles. Then click a role (to highlight it) and one or more users (to highlight them), and then click Add User(s) to Role. This invokes the AddUsers_OnClick event handler.

First you check to make sure a role has been selected:

```
if (RolesListBox.SelectedItem == null)
{
    Msg.Text = "Please select a role.";
    return;
}
```

and that at least one user has been selected:

```
if (UsersListBox.SelectedItem == null)
{
    Msg.Text = "Please select one or more users.";
    return;
}
```

Then you get an array of the users to be added:

```
string[ ] newusers = new string[UsersListBox.GetSelectedIndices( ).
Length];
```

and you iterate through those users, retrieving each selected user's name:

```
for (int i = 0; i < newusers.Length; i++)
{
    newusers[i] = UsersListBox.Items[
        UsersListBox.GetSelectedIndices( )[i]].Value;
}
```

Now you call the static AddUsersToRole method on the Roles class, passing in the array of usernames and the role you want these users added to. Then you rebind the users who are in that role to the UsersInRoleGrid method:

```
try
{
    Roles.AddUsersToRole(newusers, RolesListBox.SelectedItem.Value);

    // Re-bind users in role to GridView.

    usersInRole = Roles.GetUsersInRole(RolesListBox.SelectedItem.Value);
    UsersInRoleGrid.DataSource = usersInRole;
    UsersInRoleGrid.DataBind( );
}
catch (HttpException e)
{
    Msg.Text = e.Message;
}
```

The results are shown in Figure 4-24.

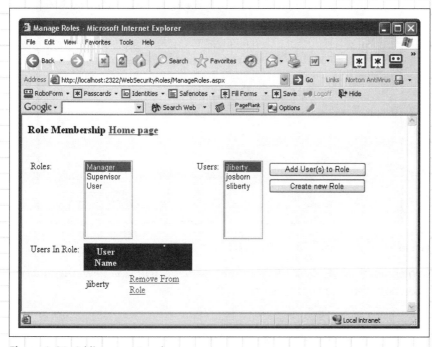

Figure 4-24. Adding users to roles

Add each user to one or more roles, and when you are done you'll be ready to test whether these roles have any effect. To do so, stop the application and edit the default page. Click the smart tag for the Login-View control and click Edit RoleGroups, as shown in Figure 4-25. This will open the RoleGroup Collection Editor dialog box.

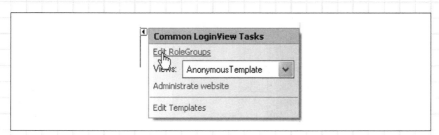

Figure 4-25. Clicking Edit RoleGroups

Add a couple of the roles you created earlier, as shown in Figure 4-26.

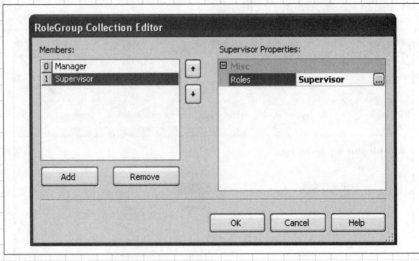

Figure 4-26. The RoleGroup Collection Editor

Switch to Source view on your *Default.aspx* page; a new section has been added to the LoginView control:

```
<asp:LoginView ID="LoginView1" Runat="server">
    <RoleGroups>
        <asp:RoleGroup Roles="Manager"></asp:RoleGroup>
        <asp:RoleGroup Roles="Supervisor"></asp:RoleGroup>
    </RoleGroups>
```

Now you can control what the members of each role will see by using contentTemplate elements. You add these between the opening and closing tags of each role:

```
<RoleGroups>
    <asp:RoleGroup Roles="Manager">
        <ContentTemplate>
          Welcome
          <asp:LoginName ID="LoginNameManager" Runat="server" />
          You are a manager
        </ContentTemplate>
    </asp:RoleGroup>
    <asp:RoleGroup Roles="Supervisor">
        <ContentTemplate>
            Supervisor tools go here
        </ContentTemplate>
    </asp:RoleGroup>
</RoleGroups>
```

Run the application. In the preceding example, I added josborn and sliberty to the Supervisor role, but not jliberty, who is in the Manager role. When I log in as josborn I see the words "Supervisor tools go here," but if I log in as jliberty I do not see those words. Instead, I see the words dictated by the content template associated with managers.

What about...

...restricting access to pages based on roles? Can I do that?

Yes, you can test if the logged-in user is in a particular role by using the `User.IsInRole` method:

```
bool isManager = User.IsInRole("Manager");
```

You can also restrict access by adding an authorization section to a *Web. config* file (which you can place in a subdirectory to control access to all files in that subdirectory and to all of its subdirectories), and you can use the `location` element to control access to specific files:

```
<authorization>
  <deny users='?' />
  <allow roles='Manager' />
  <deny users='*' />
</authorization>
```

The first line (`deny users='?'`) prohibits access to anyone who is not logged in. The second line (`allow roles='Manager'`) allows access to anyone in the Manager role, and the final line (`deny users='*'`) disallows anyone, but is overridden by `allow roles`.

...what about using the ASP.NET Web Site Administration Tool to set up roles?

Sure! First you need to stop the application. Then, on the Visual Studio menu bar, click Website → ASP.NET Configuration and choose the Security tab. Click "Enable roles," as shown in Figure 4-27.

Where can I learn more?

MSDN offers a good article on membership, titled "New Membership Features in ASP.NET Whidbey." Also, see my article on roles, titled "ASP.NET Forms Security Part 2" and available on O'Reilly's ONDotnet.com site at *http://www.ondotnet.com*. You'll also find an excellent article on roles and ASP.NET 2.0 security by Alex Homer, Rob Howard, and David Sussman at *http://www.informit.com/articles/article.asp?p=351414&seqNum=3*.

Create Personalized Web Sites

Modern web sites that are designed to be visited by users repeatedly should support personalization for those users. Personalization enables the site to remember the user's preferences and, if appropriate, previous user choices (for example, "You have three items in your shopping cart.")

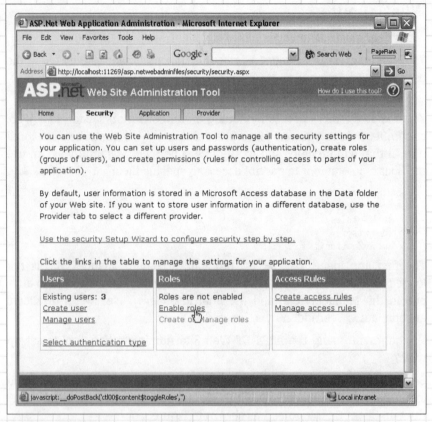

Figure 4-27. Enabling roles through the ASP.NET Web Site Administration Tool

---

TIP

ASP.NET provides extensive support for personalization, allowing your site to "remember" your user's preferences.

How do I do that?

To get started, you'll want a new project that duplicates the work you accomplished in the previous lab. Here are the steps you need to take:

1. Create a new web site and name it `SitePersonalization`.
2. On the Visual Studio menu bar, choose Website → Copy Website and click the Connect to Website button. The relevant part of the page is shown in Figure 4-28.

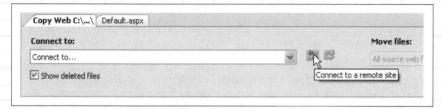

Figure 4-28. Connecting to a remote site

3. Point to the previous lab and click Open. The wizard uses a question mark to identify the files that have the same name in both applications. Highlight all the files in the remote site, and then click the left-pointing arrow, as shown in Figure 4-29.

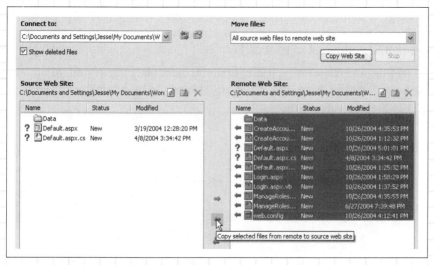

Figure 4-29. Copying all files from the remote web site to the source web site

4. Close the wizard and, if prompted, click Yes to overwrite files and Yes to update files.

TIP

If you did not create the previous lab, you can access the files by downloading the source code and copying it from the *SecurityRoles* folder.

Run the program to make sure you have a duplicate of your previous lab.

The simplest form of personalization is to record information about the user, and then to make that information available whenever the user logs on. This requires a kind of persistence that goes beyond session state. To create true personalization, you'll want to store the user's choices and information in a database that associates the saved information with a particular user, and that persists indefinitely.

ASP.NET 2.0 provides all the plumbing required. You do not have to design, edit, or manage the database tables; all of that is done for you.

ASP.NET 2.0 has decoupled the Profile API (how you programmatically interact with profile data) from the underlying data provider (how you store the data). This allows you to use the default provider (SQL Server Express), or one of the other providers supplied (SQL Server), or even to write your own provider (for example, for an existing customer relationship management system), without changing the way you interact with the profile in the rest of your code.

To add data to the user's profile, first you must alert the system about the data you want to store. You do so in *Web.config* by adding a profile section to the system.web element:

```xml
<?xml version="1.0"?>
<configuration>
    <connectionStrings>
    <remove name="LocalSqlServer" />
    <add name="LocalSqlServer" connectionString="data source=.\
sqlexpress;Integrated Security=SSPI;Initial Catalog=aspnetdb" />
    </connectionStrings>
    <system.web>
        <membership defaultProvider="AspNetSqlMembershipProvider" />
    <authentication mode="Forms"/>
        <roleManager enabled="True" defaultProvider="AspNetSqlRoleProvider" />
        <compilation debug="true"/>
        <profile>
            <properties>
                <add name="lastName" />
                <add name="firstName" />
                <add name="phoneNumber" />
                <add name="birthDate" type="System.DateTime"/>
            </properties>
        </profile>

    </system.web>
</configuration>
```

This causes the Profile API to create storage for four pieces of information: first and last name, phone number, and birth date. The default storage type is string. Notice, however, that we are storing the birth date as a DateTime object.

You can gather this information in any way you want. To keep the example simple, we'll remove the role groups section from *Default.aspx* and add a new hyperlink to `LoggedInTemplate`:

```
<asp:LoginView ID="LoginView1" Runat="server">
    <LoggedInTemplate>
        Welcome
        <asp:LoginName ID="LoginName1" Runat="server" />
        <asp:HyperLink ID="linkProfile" Runat="server"
            NavigateUrl="~/ProfileInfo.aspx">Add Profile Info
        </asp:HyperLink>
        ...
    </LoggedInTemplate>
    ...
</asp:LoginView>
```

As you can see, the link brings you to *ProfileInfo.aspx*, a page you'll create now. Add a table, and within the table add labels and checkboxes as well as a Save button, as shown in Figure 4-30.

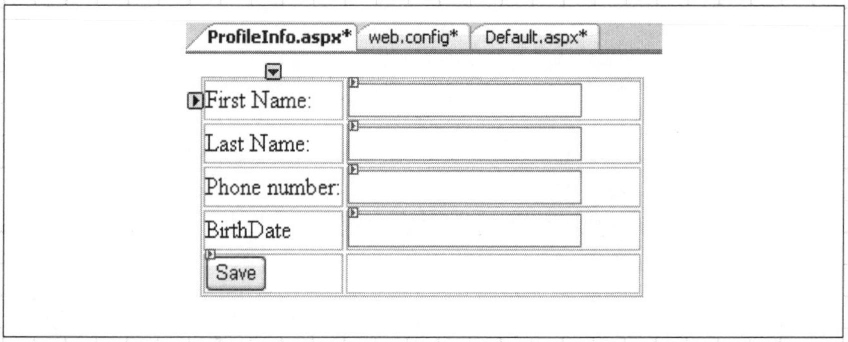

Figure 4-30. The Profile table

The HTML code for the Profile table is shown in Example 4-3.

Example 4-3. HTML for the Profile table

```
<%@ Page Language="C#" AutoEventWireup="true" CodeFile="ProfileInfo.aspx.cs"
Inherits="ProfileInfo_aspx" %>

<!DOCTYPE html PUBLIC "-//W3C//DTD XHTML 1.1//EN" "http://www.w3.org/TR/xhtml11/
DTD/xhtml11.dtd">

<html xmlns="http://www.w3.org/1999/xhtml" >
<head runat="server">
    <title>Profile Information</title>
</head>
<body>
    <form id="form1" runat="server">
    <div>
        <table>
```

Example 4-3. HTML for the Profile table (continued)

```
            <tr>
                <td>First Name: </td>
                <td style="width: 193px">
                  <asp:TextBox ID="firstName" Runat="server" />
                </td>
            </tr>
            <tr>
                <td>Last Name: </td>
                <td style="width: 193px">
                 <asp:TextBox ID="lastName" Runat="server" /></td>
<!--            <td>
                    <asp:RequiredFieldValidator ID="lastNameRequired"
Runat="server" ErrorMessage="Last name is required" ControlToValidate="lastName"
Display="Dynamic">
                    *</asp:RequiredFieldValidator>
                </td>
-->
            </tr>
            <tr>
                <td>Phone number: </td>
                <td style="width: 193px">
                    <asp:TextBox ID="phone" Runat="server" />
                </td>
            </tr>
            <tr>
                <td>BirthDate</td>
                <td style="width: 193px"><asp:TextBox ID="birthDate"
Runat="server" /></td>
            </tr>
             <tr>
                <td>
                    <asp:Button ID="save" Text="Save" Runat="server"
                        OnClick="save_Click" />
                </td>
                <td style="width: 193px"></td>
            </tr>
        </table>
    </div>
         
    </form>
</body>
</html>
```

All you have to do now is add an event handler for the Save button:

```
void save_Click(object sender, EventArgs e)
{
    if (Profile.IsAnonymous == false)
    {
        Profile.lastName = this.lastName.Text;
        Profile.firstName = this.firstName.Text;
        Profile.phoneNumber = this.phone.Text;
```

```
        Profile.birthDate = Convert.ToDateTime(this.birthDate.Text);
    }
    Response.Redirect("Default.aspx");
}
```

When you start the application, you are asked to log in. Once you do this, a new hyperlink, Add Profile Info appears. This was created by the hyperlink you added to `LoggedInTemplate` (earlier). Clicking that link brings you to your new Profile page.

The `Profile` object has properties that correspond to the properties you added in *Web.config*. To test that the `Profile` object has in fact stored this data, you'll add a panel to the bottom of the default page, after the hyperlinks but before the closing `</div>` tag:

```
<asp:Panel ID="pnlInfo" Runat="server" Visible="False" Width="422px"
Height="63px">
  <br />
  <table width="100%">
    <tr>
      <td>
        <asp:Label ID="lblFullName" Runat="server"
         Text="Full name unknown">
        </asp:Label></td>
    </tr>
    <tr>
      <td>
        <asp:Label ID="lblPhone" Runat="server"
         Text="Phone number unknown">
        </asp:Label>
      </td>
    </tr>
    <tr>
      <td>
        <asp:Label ID="lblBirthDate" Runat="server"
          Text="Birthdate unknown">
        </asp:Label>
      </td>
    </tr>
  </table>
</asp:Panel>
```

The panel has a table with three rows, and each row has a label that is initialized to say that the value is unknown (this is not normally needed, but it's included here to ensure that the data you see was in fact retrieved from the `Profile` object). When the page is loaded, you check to see if you have profile data for this user and, if so, you assign that data to the appropriate controls:

```
public partial class Default_aspx
{
    public void Page_Load(object sender, EventArgs e)
    {
```

```
if (Profile.UserName != null && Profile.IsAnonymous == false)
{
    this.lblFullName.Text = "Full name: " +
        Profile.firstName + " " + Profile.lastName;
    this.lblPhone.Text = "Phone: " + Profile.phoneNumber;
    this.lblBirthDate.Text = "Born: " +
      Profile.birthDate.ToShortDateString();
    this.pnlInfo.Visible = true;
}
else
{
    this.pnlInfo.Visible = false;
}
}      // end page load
}        // end partial class
```

Notice that you convert DateTime to a string for easy display in the label.

Run the application, log in, and click Add Profile Info. You will be brought to the Profile Information form, as shown in Figure 4-31.

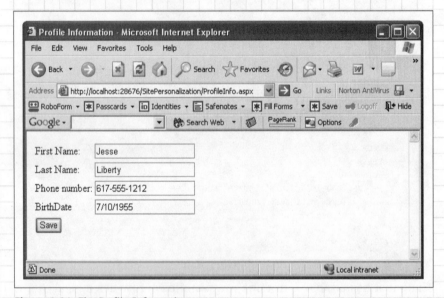

Figure 4-31. The Profile Information page

When you return to the default page, the Page_Load event fires, both parts of the if statement return true (that is, the UserName value in the profile is not null), and the user is logged in and thus is not anonymous:

```
if (Profile.UserName != null && Profile.IsAnonymous == false)
```

Your profile information is displayed, as shown in Figure 4-32.

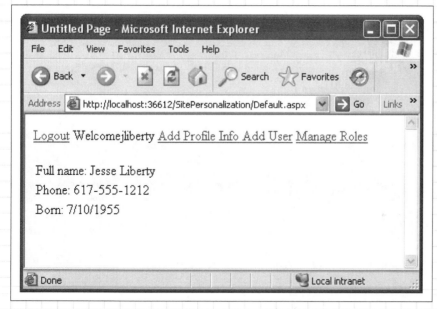

Figure 4-32. Profile information displayed

What about...

...the profile information? Where is it stored?

To see where the profile information is stored, stop the application and examine the tables in your storage database. You'll want to examine two tables: aspnet_Users (which lists all the users your security system knows about) and aspnet_Profile (which lists the profile information for those users), as shown in Figure 4-33.

There are a number of things to notice. I've circled the UserID in both tables; the entries in the Profile table are matched to the individual user via the UserID.

The Profile table has two significant columns in addition to UserID: PropertyNames and PropertyValueString. The entries in the PropertyNames columns correspond to the entries you created in the <profile> section of *Web.config*:

```
<profile>
    <properties>
        <add name="lastName" />
        <add name="firstName" />
        <add name="phoneNumber" />
        <add name="birthDate" type="System.DateTime"/>
    </properties>
</profile>
```

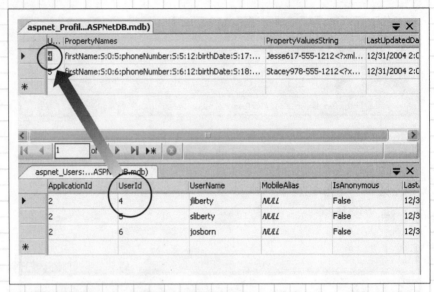

Figure 4-33. Examining the profile in the database

Notice that birthDate is listed as a string that begins at offset 24 and is 95 characters long, but if you look at the PropertyValuesString column, you'll find that the birth date is encoded as XML.

Commercial sites often have to store complex user-defined types (classes) or collections for individual users (for example, shopping carts).

Each property is named (for example, lastName) and is given a type (S for string), a starting offset (firstName begins at offset 7), and a length (firstName's value has a length of 5). This offset and value are used to find the value within the PropertyValueString field.

...what about saving complex types?

So far you've seen how to save built-in types such as strings and dates. In the next lab you'll see how to store complex types that might be needed to create a "shopping cart."

Where can I learn more?

O'Reilly's ONDotnet site *(http://www.ondotnet.com)* provides numerous articles on personalization and extensive documentation on the subject is available in the MSDN.

Personalize with Complex Types

Although personalizing a site for your users is terrific, to make a useful commercial site you often have to store complex user-defined types (classes) or collections. The ASP.NET Web Site Administration Tool (WAT) makes that easy.

How do I do that?

Once again you need a new web site. Create one and call it ComplexPersonalization. Use the Copy Web Site Wizard to copy the previous lab to a new lab, or download the source from the previous lab and copy it to a new lab from the *SitePersonalization* folder.

In this lab you'll create the world's simplest shopping cart.

To create a complex profile property you'll need to edit the *Web.config* file. In this case, we'll add a collection of strings called CHOSENBOOKS that will allow the user to choose one or more books and have those choices stored in the profile.

Add a line to *Web.config* for your new property:

```
<profile>
  <properties>
    <add name="lastName" />
    <add name="firstName" />
    <add name="phoneNumber" />
    <add name="birthDate" type="System.DateTime"/>
    <add name="CHOSENBOOKS"
      type="System.Collections.Specialized.StringCollection" />
  </properties>
</profile>
```

To see this collection at work, drag a CheckBoxList from the Visual Studio Toolbox onto the *ProfileInfo* page, which you will populate with the names of four books. Hand-populate this list by clicking the Items property and filling in the ListItems Collection Editor, or by adding the control by hand to the *.aspx* page using the following code:

```
<td style="width: 193px">
    <asp:CheckBoxList ID="cblBooks" Runat="server" >
        <asp:ListItem>Programming C#</asp:ListItem>
        <asp:ListItem>Programming ASP.NET</asp:ListItem>
        <asp:ListItem>Programming .NET Apps</asp:ListItem>
        <asp:ListItem>Programming VB.NET</asp:ListItem>
    </asp:CheckBoxList>
</td>
```

Click the Save button; the handler will add the books to the profile:

```
void save_Click(object sender, EventArgs e)
{
    Profile.lastName = this.lastName.Text;
    Profile.firstName = this.firstName.Text;
    Profile.phoneNumber = this.phone.Text;
    Profile.birthDate = Convert.ToDateTime(this.birthDate.Text);

    Profile.CHOSENBOOKS = new System.Collections.Specialized.
StringCollection();
    foreach (ListItem item in this.cblBooks.Items)
```

```
        {
            if (item.Selected)
            {
                Profile.CHOSENBOOKS.Add(item.Value.ToString( ));
            }
        }
        Response.Redirect("Default.aspx");
    }
```

TIP

Each time you save the books, you create an instance of the String collection, and then you iterate through the checked listboxes, looking for the selected items. Each selected item is added to the String collection within the profile (the CHOSENBOOKS property).

To confirm that this data has been stored, add a listbox (lbBooks) to the *Default.aspx* page, and bind that listbox to the collection in the profile:

```
public partial class Default_aspx : System.Web.UI.Page
{
    protected void Page_Load(object sender, EventArgs e)
    {
        if (Profile.UserName != null && Profile.IsAnonymous == false)
        {
            this.lblFullName.Text = "Full name: " +
                Profile.firstName + " " + Profile.lastName;
          .this.lblPhone.Text = "Phone: " + Profile.phoneNumber;
            this.lblBirthDate.Text = "Born: " +
                Profile.birthDate.ToShortDateString( );
            this.pnlInfo.Visible = true;
        }
        else
        {
            this.pnlInfo.Visible = false;
        }

        if (Profile.CHOSENBOOKS != null)
        {
            this.lbBooks.DataSource = Profile.CHOSENBOOKS;
            this.lbBooks.DataBind( );
            this.lbBooks.Visible = true;
        }
        else
        {
            this.lbBooks.Visible = false;
        }
    }
```

To make your code a bit easier to maintain, you want to have the selected values (name, phone, selected books, etc.) prefilled when you return to the Profile Information page, so you'll implement a bit of code on Page_Load to get the initial values from the Profile object:

```
public partial class ProfileInfo_aspx : System.Web.UI.Page
{
    protected void Page_Load(object sender, EventArgs e)
    {
      if (!IsPostBack && Profile.UserName != null)
      {
        if (Profile.IsAnonymous == false)
        {
          this.lastName.Text = Profile.lastName;
          this.firstName.Text = Profile.firstName;
          this.phone.Text = Profile.phoneNumber;
          this.birthDate.Text = Profile.birthDate.ToShortDateString();
        }

        if (Profile.CHOSENBOOKS != null)
        {
          foreach (ListItem li in this.cblBooks.Items)
          {
            foreach (string s in Profile.CHOSENBOOKS)
            {
              if (li.Text == s)
              {
                li.Selected = true;
            }   // end if text is the same
          }     // end foreach string in saved isbns
        }       // end foreach item in the listbox
      }         // end if savedisbns not null
    }           // end if not postback
  }             // end Page Load
}
```

Each time you navigate to the Profile Information page, the values are updated from the existing profile (if any) and you are free to change them and save the changes, as shown in Figure 4-34.

When you return to the default page, your saved profile information is reflected, as shown in Figure 4-35.

What about...

...anonymous personalization?

Most sites would like to allow the user to make choices (for example, add to a shopping cart) *before* logging in. In this lab that is not possible, but anonymous personalization is covered in the next lab.

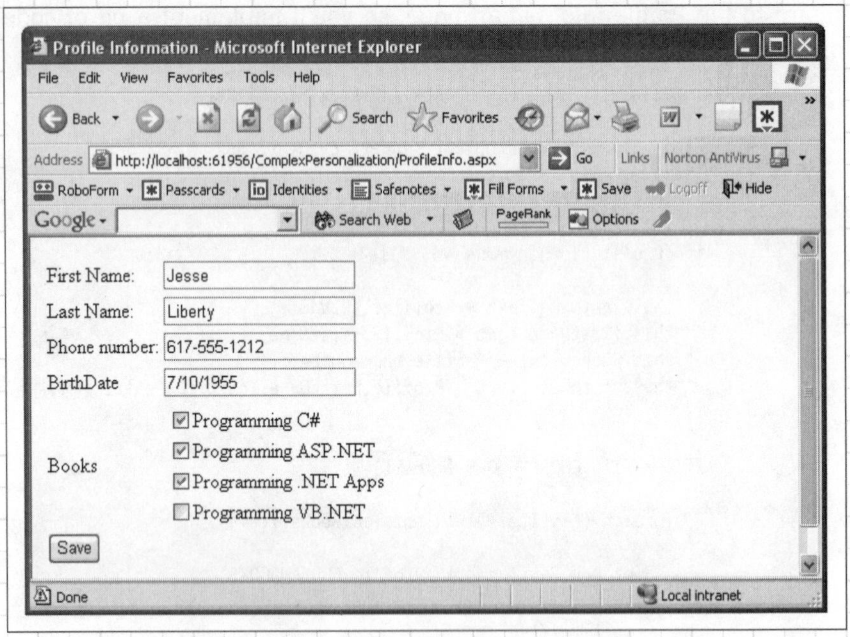

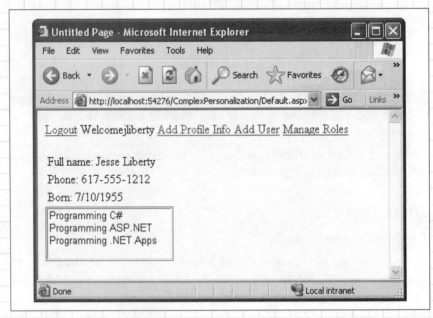

Figure 4-34. Profile information with "shopping cart"

Figure 4-35. Shopping-cart choices in profile

Where can I learn more?

Numerous articles on personalization are available on ONDotnet (*http://www.ondotnet.com*), as well as in the MSDN.

Add Anonymous Personalization to Your Site

It is common to allow your users to personalize your site before identifying themselves. A classic example of this is Amazon.com, which lets you add books to your shopping cart *before* you log in (you need to log in only to actually purchase what is in your cart).

ASP.NET 2.0 supports personalization and, even more important, the ability to link the anonymous data with a user's personalized data once that user logs in (you don't want the user to lose what is in his cart when he does log in).

It is common practice to allow users to personalize your site before identifying themselves.

How do I do that?

Once again, use Copy Web Site to copy the previous lab to a new web site called AnonymousPersonalization.

To enable anonymous personalization you must update your *Web.config* file:

```
<?xml version="1.0"?>
<configuration>
  <system.web>
      <anonymousIdentification enabled="true" />
    <authentication mode="Forms"/>
      <roleManager enabled="true"/>
      <compilation debug="true"/>
        <profile>
            <properties>
                <add name="lastName" />
                <add name="firstName" />
                <add name="phoneNumber" />
                <add name="birthDate" type="System.DateTime" />
                <add name="CHOSENBOOKS"
                  type="System.Collections.Specialized.StringCollection"
                  allowAnonymous="true" />
            </properties>
        </profile>

  </system.web>
</configuration>
```

Add the attribute-value pair allowAnonymous="true" to the CHOSENBOOKS element of *Web.config*.

Redesign your *Default.aspx* page so that both the hyperlink that links to the Profile Information page and the lbBooks listbox are outside of the LoginView control (so you can see the hyperlink and the list, even if you are not logged in). While you are at it, rename Add Profile Info to Profile Info because you will be using this link to add and edit the profile information, as shown in Example 4-4.

Example 4-4. Modified Default.aspx

```
<%@ Page Language="C#" AutoEventWireup="true" CodeFile="Default.aspx.cs"
Inherits="Default_aspx" %>

<!DOCTYPE html PUBLIC "-//W3C//DTD XHTML 1.1//EN" "http://www.w3.org/TR/xhtml11/
DTD/xhtml11.dtd">

<html xmlns="http://www.w3.org/1999/xhtml" >
<head runat="server">
    <title>Untitled Page</title>
</head>
<body>
    <form id="form1" runat="server">
    <div>
        <asp:LoginStatus ID="LoginStatus1" Runat="server" />
        <asp:LoginView ID="LoginView1" Runat="server" >

            <LoggedInTemplate>
                Welcome
                 <asp:LoginName ID="LoginName1" Runat="server" />

            </LoggedInTemplate>
            <AnonymousTemplate>
                 You are not yet logged in
            </AnonymousTemplate>
        </asp:LoginView>
        <asp:HyperLink ID="HyperLink1" Runat="server" NavigateUrl="~/AddUser.
aspx">Add User</asp:HyperLink>
        <asp:HyperLink ID="HyperLink2" Runat="server" NavigateUrl="~/ManageRoles.
aspx">Manage Roles</asp:HyperLink>
        <asp:Panel ID="pnlInfo" Runat="server" Visible="False" Width="422px"
Height="63px">
            <br />
            <table width="100%">
                <tr><td><asp:Label ID="lblFullName" Runat="server"  Text="Full
name unknown"></asp:Label></td></tr>
                <tr><td><asp:Label ID="lblPhone" Runat="server" Text="Phone
number unknown"></asp:Label></td></tr>
                <tr><td><asp:Label ID="lblBirthDate" Runat="server"
Text="Birthdate  unknown"></asp:Label></td></tr>
            </table>
```

Example 4-4. Modified Default.aspx (continued)

```
        </asp:Panel>

    <asp:HyperLink ID="linkProfile" Runat="server"
            NavigateUrl="~/ProfileInfo.aspx">Profile Info</asp:HyperLink>

        <br />  <asp:ListBox ID="lbBooks" Runat="server" />

    </div>
    </form>
</body>
</html>
```

When an anonymous user chooses books, the user will automatically be assigned a Globally Unique Identifier (GUID), and an entry will be made in the database for that ID. However, note that only those properties marked with allowAnonymous can be stored, so you must modify your save_Click event handler in *ProfileInfo.aspx.cs*. Bracket the entries for all the profile elements *except* CHOSENBOOKS in an if statement that tests whether the user is currently Anonymous, as shown in the following snippet:

```
if (Profile.IsAnonymous == false)
{
    Profile.lastName = this.lastName.Text;
    Profile.firstName = this.firstName.Text;
    Profile.phoneNumber = this.phone.Text;
    Profile.birthDate = Convert.ToDateTime(this.birthDate.Text);
}
Profile.CHOSENBOOKS =
    new System.Collections.Specialized.StringCollection();
```

When saving your profile data, you check whether the IsAnonymous property is false. If it is false, you know you are dealing with a logged-in user, and you can get all the properties; otherwise, you can get only those that are allowed for anonymous users.

Before you run the application, however, you must enable the anonymous identification feature. To do so, add the following attribute-value pair to the top of your *Web.config* file:

```
<anonymousIdentification enabled="true" />
```

Run the application. Do *not* log in, but do click the Profile Info link. Select a few books and click Save. When you return to the default page, you are still not logged in, but your selected books are displayed, as shown in Figure 4-36.

Stop the application and reopen the database. You'll see that an ID has been created for this anonymous user and UserName has been set to the GUID generated. In addition, the shopping cart has been stored in the corresponding record, as shown in Figure 4-37.

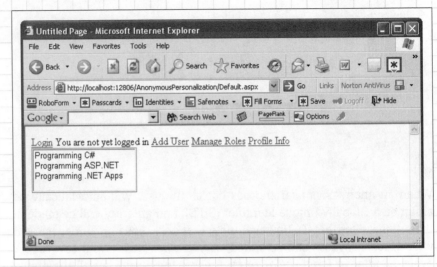

Figure 4-36. Book list for anonymous user

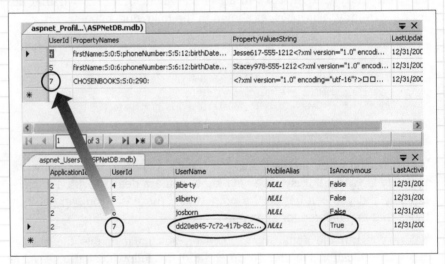

Figure 4-37. Anonymous User record in database

What about...

...migrating the anonymous data to the actual user's data?

When the user does log in, you must migrate the profile data you've accumulated for the anonymous user to the appropriate authenticated user's record (so that, for example, shopping cart items are not lost). You do this by writing a global handler in *global.asax*.

If your project does not yet have a *global.asax* file, right-click the project and choose Add New Item. One of your choices will be Global Application Class, and it will automatically be named *global.asax*. Within that class, add a method to handle the MigrateAnonymous event that is fired when a user logs in, as shown in the following snippet:

```
void Profile_MigrateAnonymous(object sender, ProfileMigrateEventArgs e)
{
  ASP.HttpProfile anonymousProfile = Profile.GetProfile(e.AnonymousId);
  if (anonymousProfile != null && anonymousProfile.CHOSENBOOKS != null)
  {
    foreach (string s in anonymousProfile.CHOSENBOOKS)
    {
      Profile.CHOSENBOOKS.Remove(s);  // avoid duplicates
      Profile.CHOSENBOOKS.Add(s);
    }
  }
}
```

The first step in this method is to get a reference to the profile that matches the AnonymousID that is passed in as a property of the ProfileMigrateEventArgs structure:

```
ASP.HttpProfile anonymousProfile = Profile.GetProfile(e.AnonymousId);
```

If the reference is not null, you know there is a matching anonymous profile, and you can pick up whatever data you need from that profile. In this case, copy over the CHOSENBOOKS collection.

To associate anonymous data with a user who has decided to log in, you must write a global handler in global.asax.

The user's profile is updated, and the books chosen by the anonymous user are now part of that user's profile, as shown in Figure 4-38.

Where can I learn more?

For more information, see my article "Personalization in ASP.NET 2.0" on ONDotnet (*http://www.ondotnet.com*), as well as the article "Personalization with ASP.NET 2.0" by Patel et. al, in the MSDN Library.

Let Users Personalize Your Site with Themes

Themes allow your users to personalize the look and feel of your site's controls.

Many users like to personalize their favorite web sites, by setting the look and feel of the site's controls to meet their own personal aesthetic. ASP.NET 2.0 provides support for themes that enable you to offer that level of personalization to your users.

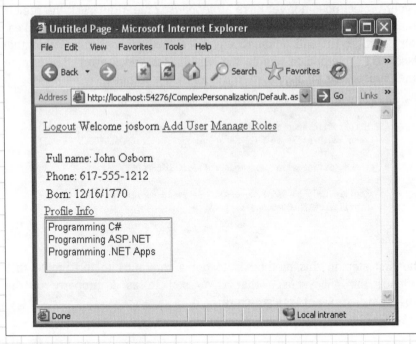

Figure 4-38. Profiles merged

How do I do that?

A *theme* is a collection of skins. A *skin* describes how a control should look. A skin can define stylesheet attributes, images, colors, and so forth.

Having multiple themes allows your users to choose how they want your site to look by switching from one set of skins to another at the touch of a button. Combined with personalization, your site can remember the look and feel your user prefers.

Themes come in two flavors. The first, called a *stylesheet theme*, defines styles that the page or control can override. These are, essentially, equivalent to CSS stylesheets. The second type, called a *customization theme*, cannot be overridden. You set a stylesheet theme by adding the StyleSheetTheme attribute to the page directive, and similarly, you set a customization theme by setting the Theme attribute in the page directive.

In any given page, the properties for the controls are set in this order:

- Properties are applied first from a stylesheet theme.
- Properties are then overridden based on properties set in the control.
- Properties are then overridden based on a customization theme.

Thus, the customization theme is guaranteed to have the final word in determining the control's look and feel.

Skins also come in two flavors: default skins and explicitly named skins. Thus, you might create a *Labels* skin file with this declaration:

```
<asp:Label runat="server"
ForeColor="Blue" Font-Size="Large"
Font-Bold="True" Font-Italic="True" />
```

This is a default skin for all label controls. It looks like the definition of an ASP:Label control, but it is housed in a skin file and thus is used to define the look and feel of all Label objects.

In addition, however, you might decide that some labels must be red. To accomplish this, you create a second skin, but you assign this skin a SkinID attribute:

```
<asp:Label runat="server" SkinID="RedLabel"
ForeColor="Red" Font-Size="Large"
Font-Bold="True" Font-Italic="True" />
```

Any label that does not have a SkinID attribute will get the default skin, and any label that sets SkinID ="Red" will get your named skin.

Here are the steps to providing a personalized web site:

1. Create the test site.
2. Organize your themes and skins.
3. Enable themes and skins for your site.
4. Specify themes declaratively or programmatically.

Create the test site

To demonstrate the use of themes and skins, once again we'll build on the personalization labs we've been incrementally improving throughout this chapter. Use the Copy Web Site page to create a new web site, and name it ThemesandSkins.

TIP

If you are starting here without having done the previous labs, create a new application named ThemesandSkins, and download and copy in the source from the *ComplexPersonalization* folder as a starting point.

To begin your new application you'll need some controls for which you can set the look and feel. Open *Default.aspx* and add controls to the page, using the code shown in Example 4-5.

Example 4-5. Controls for demonstrating skins

```
<table width ="100%">
        <tr>
            <td >
                <asp:HyperLink ID="linkProfile" Runat="server"
                NavigateUrl="~/ProfileInfo.aspx">
                 Profile Info</asp:HyperLink>
            </td>
            <td >
                <asp:ListBox ID="lbBooks" Runat="server" />
            </td>
        </tr>
        <tr>
            <td >
                <asp:Label ID="lblListBox" Runat="server" Text="ListBox"/>
            </td>
            <td >
                <asp:ListBox ID="lbItems" Runat="server">
                    <asp:ListItem>First Item</asp:ListItem>
                    <asp:ListItem>Second Item</asp:ListItem>
                    <asp:ListItem>Third Item</asp:ListItem>
                    <asp:ListItem>Fourth Item</asp:ListItem>
                </asp:ListBox>
            </td>
            <td >
                <asp:Label ID="lblRadioButtonList" Runat="server"
                Text="Radio Button List"/>
            </td>
            <td >
                <asp:RadioButtonList ID="RadioButtonList1" Runat="server">
                    <asp:ListItem>Radio Button 1</asp:ListItem>
                    <asp:ListItem>Radio Button 2</asp:ListItem>
                    <asp:ListItem>Radio Button 3</asp:ListItem>
                    <asp:ListItem>Radio Button 4</asp:ListItem>
                    <asp:ListItem>Radio Button 5</asp:ListItem>
                    <asp:ListItem>Radio Button 6</asp:ListItem>
                </asp:RadioButtonList><br />
            </td>
        </tr>
          <tr>
            <td>
                <asp:Label ID="lblCalendar" Runat="server"
                 Text="Calendar"></asp:Label>
            </td>
            <td>
                <asp:Calendar ID="Calendar1" Runat="server" />
            </td>
            <td>
                <asp:Label ID="lblTextBox" Runat="server"
                 Text="TextBox"/>
            </td>
            <td>
                <asp:TextBox ID="TextBox1" Runat="server"/>
```

Example 4-5. *Controls for demonstrating skins (continued)*

```
            </td>
        </tr>
    </table>
```

Now you want to set skins that will change the look and feel of these controls, and you want to organize those skins into themes.

Organize site themes and skins

Themes are stored in your project in a folder named *App_Themes*. To create this folder, go to the Solution Explorer, right-click the project folder, and choose Add Folder → Theme Folder. Name the new folder *Dark Blue*. The *App_Themes* folder will be created automatically, with a theme folder named *Dark Blue* immediately under it. Create a second theme folder, named *Psychedelic*.

Right-click the *Dark Blue* theme folder and choose Add New Item. From the template list choose Skin File and name the file *Button.skin* (to hold all the button skins for your Dark Blue theme), as shown in Figure 4-39.

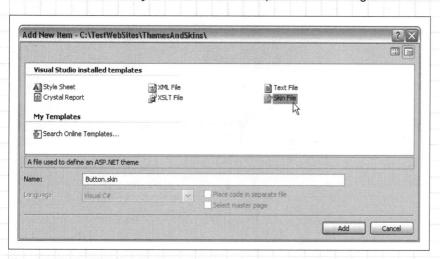

Figure 4-39. *Creating the skin file*

Each skin file is just a text file that contains a definition for the control type, but with no ID. Thus, for example, your *Label.skin* file might look like this (for the Dark Blue theme):

```
<asp:Label Runat="server"
ForeColor="Blue" Font-Size="Large"
Font-Bold="True" Font-Italic="True" />
```

Create skin files for each of the following types in both themes:

- *Button.skin*
- *Calendar.skin*
- *Label.skin*
- *ListBox.skin*
- *RadioButton.skin*
- *Text.skin*

At this point your solution should look more or less like Figure 4-40.

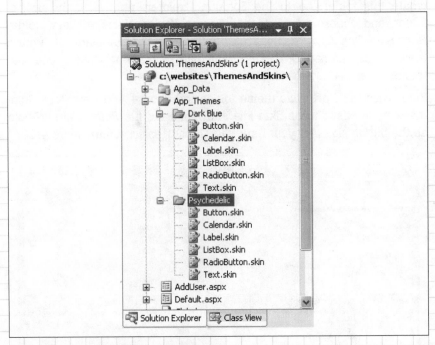

Figure 4-40. Themes and skins in your project

Enable themes and skins

To let your users choose the theme they like and have it stored in their profile, you need to add a single line to the <properties> element in the <profile> element of *Web.config*:

```
<add name="Theme" />
```

Specify themes

You can set the themes on your page either declaratively or programmatically. To set a theme declaratively, simply add the Theme attribute to the Page directive:

```
<%@ Page Language="C#" AutoEventWireup="true"
CodeFile="Default.aspx.cs" Inherits="Default_aspx" Theme="Dark Blue"%>
```

This will set the page's theme to the Dark Blue theme you've created.

You can set the theme programmatically either by hardcoding it, or (even better) by settng it from the user's profile.

You set StyleSheet themes by overriding the StyleSheetTheme property for the page, as shown in the following code snippet:

```
public override string StyleSheetTheme
{
    get
    {
        if (Profile.IsAnonymous == false && Profile.Theme != null)
            return Profile.Theme;
        else
            return "Dark Blue";
    }

    set
    {
        Profile.Theme = value;
    }
}
```

If you are going to set a customization theme programmatically, however, you must do so from the new PreInit event handler for the page because you must set the theme before the controls are created:

```
public void Page_PreInit(object sender, EventArgs e)
{
    if ( Profile.IsAnonymous == false )
    {
        Page.Theme = Profile.Theme;
    }
}
```

This presents a bit of difficulty when you want to allow the user to change the theme at runtime. If you create a control that posts the page back with a new theme, the pre-init code runs *before* the event handler for your button that changes the theme, so by the time the theme is changed the buttons have already been drawn.

To overcome this you must, unfortunately, refresh the page again (an alternative is to post to another page). For this lab we'll add two buttons to the *ProfileInfo.aspx* page:

```
<tr>
    <td>
        <asp:Button ID="ThemeBlue" Text="Dark Blue"
            Runat="server" OnClick="Set_Theme" />
    </td>
    <td>
        <asp:Button ID="ThemePsych" Text="Psychedelic"
            Runat="server" OnClick="Set_Theme" />
    </td>
</tr>
```

Notice that the two buttons share a single Click event handler:

```
void Set_Theme(object sender, EventArgs e)
{
    Button btn = sender as Button;
    if (btn.Text == "Psychedelic")
    {
        Profile.Theme = "Psychedelic";
    }
    else
    {
        Profile.Theme = "Dark Blue";
    }
}
```

When the user is not logged on, the page's default theme will be used. Once the user sets a theme in the profile, that theme will be used. Create skins for your two themes and then run the application to see the effect of applying the themes.

What about...

....overriding themes?

You can override the theme for particular controls by using named skins.

For instance, you can set the lblRadioButtonList label to be red even in the Deep Blue theme by using a named skin. To accomplish this, create two Label skins in the *Label.skin* file within the *Deep Blue* folder:

```
<asp:Label Runat="server"
ForeColor="Blue" Font-Size="Large"
Font-Bold="True" Font-Italic="True" />

<asp:Label Runat="server" SkinID="Red"
ForeColor="Red" Font-Size="Large"
Font-Bold="True" Font-Italic="True" />
```

The first skin is the default, and the second skin is a named skin because it has a `SkinID` property set to `Red`. Open the source for *Default.aspx*, find the label you want to make red, and add the `SkinID="Red"` attribute, as shown in the following code snippet:

```
<asp:Label ID="lblRadioButtonList" Runat="server" Text="Radio Button List"
SkinID="Red"/>
```

When you log in and set your theme to Dark Blue, you'll find that the label for the Radio Button List is red, as shown in Figure 4-41 (really, it is red; I swear).

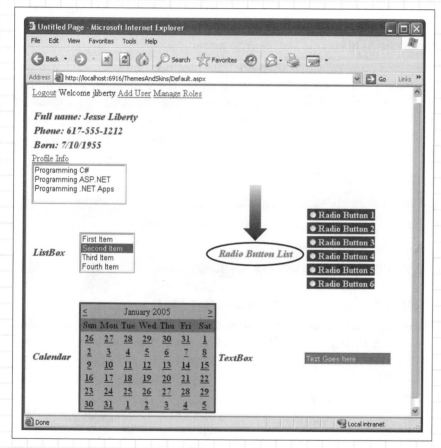

Figure 4-41. A red Radio Button List label

Where can I learn more?

For more information, see my article "Skins and Themes" on ONDotnet. com (*http://www.ondotnet.com*). In addition, the CodeGuru web site (*http://www.codeguru.com*) contains an article by Bill Evjen titled "Skins and Themes," and the 15 Seconds web site (*http://www.15seconds.com*) has an article by Thiru Thangarathinam titled "Code in Style with ASP. NET Themes." Microsoft also provides a QuickStart tutorial on themes and skins at *http://beta.asp.net/quickstart/aspnet/*.

Unify Your Look and Feel with Master Pages

Master pages provide your site with a consistent look and feel.

Web sites look better and are less confusing to users when they have a consistent "look and feel" as you move from page to page. ASP.NET 2.0 facilitates creating consistency with master pages.

A *master page* provides shared HTML, controls, and code that you can use as a template for all the pages of a site. The O'Reilly web site (*http://www.oreilly.com*) is a good example of a site that you can implement using a master page. With a master page, the logo (the O'Reilly tarsier) and an image (the O'Reilly header) can be shared across multiple pages.

How do I do that?

To see how to use master pages in this lab, follow these steps:

1. Create a new web site and add a master page.
2. Design the master page.
3. Add content pages that use the master page.

Create a new web site and add a master page

To begin, create a new web site and call it MasterPages. From the Add New Item dialog, choose Master Page, and name your master page *SiteMasterPage.master*, as shown in Figure 4-42.

Design the master page

Open the page. You'll find that an asp:contentplaceholder control has been added for you. This placeholder will be filled by the content of the pages that use this master page.

Within the master page itself you can add anything you want surrounding the asp:contentplaceholder control. Whatever you add will be replicated on all pages that use the master page.

In this example, you'll use the O'Reilly logos, provided for your use in the download files at the O'Reilly site for this book (see the Preface for

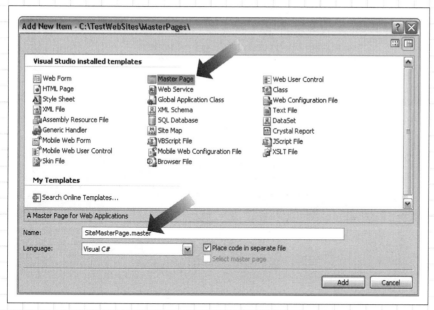

Figure 4-42. Adding a new master page

details). Create an *images* directory within your application and copy into it the *Animal.gif* and *OReillyLogo.gif* files. Then add the files to the project by right-clicking the *images* folder and choosing Add → Existing Item….

You'll place the logos and the `asp:contentplaceholder` control into a table within the *SiteMasterPage.master* file, as shown in Example 4-6.

Example 4-6. Creating the SiteMasterPage.master file with logos

```
<%@ Master Language="C#" AutoEventWireup="true"
CodeFile="SiteMastPage.master.cs" Inherits="SiteMastPage_master" %>

<!DOCTYPE html PUBLIC "-//W3C//DTD XHTML 1.1//EN" "http://www.w3.org/TR/xhtml11/
DTD/xhtml11.dtd">

<html xmlns="http://www.w3.org/1999/xhtml" >
<head runat="server">
    <title>Untitled Page</title>
</head>
<body>
    <form id="form1" runat="server">
    <div>
    <table>
        <tr>
            <td style="width: 71px; height: 127px">
                <asp:Image ID="animalLogo" Runat="server"
                ImageUrl="~/Images/Animal.gif" ImageAlign="Left" />
            </td>
```

Example 4-6. *Creating the SiteMasterPage.master file with logos (continued)*

```
            <td style="width: 423px; height: 127px">  
              <asp:Image ID="oreillyLogo" Runat="server"
              ImageUrl="~/Images/OreillyLogo.gif" ImageAlign="Bottom" /></td>
        </tr>
        <tr>
            <td colspan="2">
                <div>
                    <asp:contentplaceholder
                        id="SiteMasterPageContent"
                        runat="server">
                        If you see this content,
                        then the master page content was not replaced<br />
                    </asp:contentplaceholder>
                </div>
            </td>
        </tr>
    </table>
    </div>
    </form>
</body>
</html>
```

If you switch to Design view in Visual Studio, you'll see the master page with standard logos in place and an `asp:contentPlaceHolder` control displaying where content from other pages will be placed, as shown in Figure 4-43.

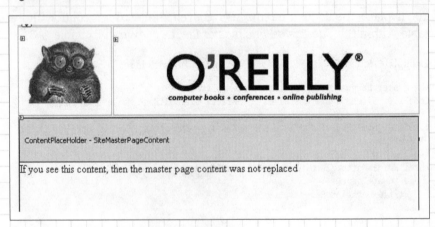

Figure 4-43. *The master page in Display view*

You can type directly into the placeholder area; in Figure 4-43, I typed in the words "If you see this content, then the master page content was not replaced."

Add content pages that use the master page

To see the master page at work, create two *.aspx* pages. Name them *Page1.aspx* and *Page2.aspx*, respectively. Create these pages as normal web pages, but check the "Select master page" checkbox, as shown in Figure 4-44. When you click Add, you'll be asked to pick which master page you want to use; so far we have selected only one.

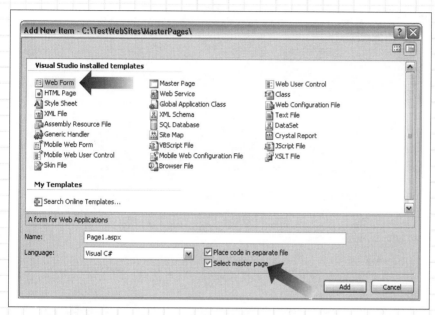

Figure 4-44. Creating the content pages

Open your new page in Design mode. You'll see exactly how the content for this new page will fit within the master page you've chosen, as shown in Figure 4-45.

TIP

Visual Studio 2005 assumes you want to use custom content. If you want to use the default content, click the smart tag and choose Default to Master's Content.

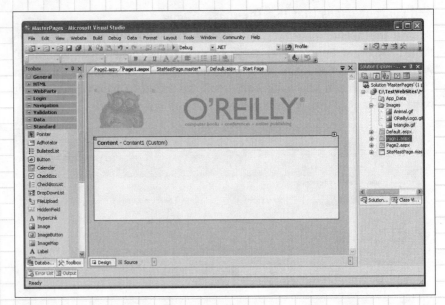

Figure 4-45. Content page within the master page

Let's add some code to *Page1.aspx* that will replace the default master content:

```
<%@ Page Language="C#" MasterPageFile="~/SiteMastPage.master"
AutoEventWireup="true" CodeFile="Page1.aspx.cs" Inherits="Page1_aspx"
Title="Untitled Page" %>

<asp:Content ID="Content1" ContentPlaceHolderID="SiteMasterPageContent"
Runat="Server">
<table>
    <tr>
        <td>
            <asp:Label ID="lblFirstName" Runat="server">First Name</asp:
Label>
        </td>
        <td>
            <asp:TextBox ID="txtFirstName" Runat="server" />
        </td>
    </tr>
    <tr>
        <td>
            <asp:Label ID="lblLastName" Runat="server">Last Name</asp:Label>
        </td>
        <td>
            <asp:TextBox ID="txtLastName" Runat="server" />
        </td>
    </tr>

</table>
</asp:Content>
```

Whatever is in the content area will be replaced by the content pages. You can place more than one asp:content-PlaceHolder control in a master page. Each has its own unique ID.

Switch to *Page2.aspx*, and this time drag a `Calendar` control onto the content area of the page. Add hyperlinks between your two pages so that you can move back and forth between them. Notice that the two pages share a common look and feel, though each page is made unique by the data and controls you placed within the `asp:contentPlaceHolder` control, as shown in Figure 4-46.

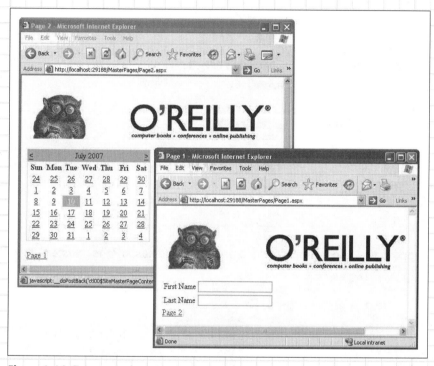

Figure 4-46. Two pages sharing a common master page

What about...

...nesting master pages within one another? Can I do that?

Yes, you can create submaster pages. To do so, create a new master page, but within the submaster set the `MasterPageFile` attribute to the parent-master page. Thus, if you create *SubMaster.master*, in the heading of *SubMaster.master* you will have a line such as this:

```
<%@ Master MasterPageFile="SiteMasterPage.master"
language ="c#" CompileWith="Submaster.master.cs"
ClassName="Submaster" %>
```

...what if I want to modify properties of the master page at runtime?

You can do that, no problem. Just reach up into the master and change it from within your content page.

Sometimes you'll want to modify the master on the fly, from within the code of the content page. To accomplish this, you must expose a property in the master page. Then you can use the (implicit) Master member field of your *.aspx* page to access that property.

TIP

You can accomplish the same thing with late-binding (FindControl( )), but this uses reflection and is slower:

```
public void Page_Load(object sender, EventArgs e)
{
    Control c = Master.FindControl("AnimalLogo");
    Image img = c as Image;
    if (img != null)
    {
            img.ImageUrl = "~//images//Triangle.gif";
    }
}
```

Suppose you add a property such as this to *SiteMasterPage_master*:

```
public Image AnimalLogo
{
    set { this.animalLogo = value; }
}
```

Now you can change the image used for animalLogo by setting that property from within a *.aspx* page. Change *Page2.aspx* to add this code:

```
public void Page_Load(object sender, EventArgs e)
{
    ((SiteMasterPage)this.Master).AnimalLogo.ImageURL = "~//images//Triangle.gif";
}
```

The result is shown in Figure 4-47. *Page2.aspx* has reached up into its master page and changed its logo. This can be very useful when implementing Emerson's advice in *Self Reliance*: "A foolish consistency is the hobgoblin of little minds."

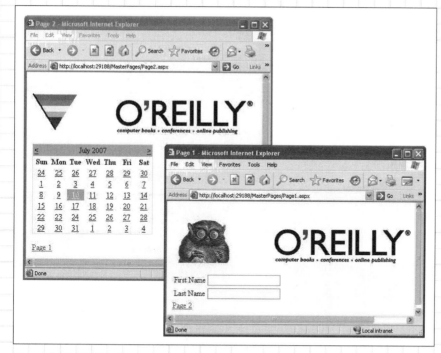

Figure 4-47. Setting the master page image

Where can I learn more?

For more information, see my article "Master Pages in ASP.NET" on ONDot-net.com (*http://www.ondotnet.com*). In addition, a very helpful QuickStart tutorial titled "Creating a Layout Using Master Pages" is available on *http://beta.asp.net/quickstart/aspnet/*.

Data

One of the stated goals of .NET 2.0 is to push more of the plumbing into the .NET Framework and to provide controls for Windows and web developers that reduce the amount of code they will write. Nowhere is this seen more profoundly than when writing code for interacting with databases.

Bind to Data Without Writing Code

In .NET 2.0 you write far less code to set up database interactions, but you do not sacrifice control when creating, displaying, updating, or deleting data. In fact, you can create a very powerful sorted, paged grid of data from your database with virtually no code at all.

How do I do that?

TIP

You will need to have Northwind installed on your database to do the labs in this chapter. If you have installed SQL Server (Developer or Production version) or Access, you already have Northwind. If you have SQL Server Express, download the appropriate setup files from the Microsoft web site (*http://www.microsoft.com*).

First, create a new web application and name it DataBindingNoCode. Click the Data tab of the Toolbox and drag a GridView control onto the default web form, *Default.aspx*.

In this chapter:
- *Bind to Data Without Writing Code*
- *Create Detail Pages*
- *Create Master Detail Records*
- *Get Database Statistics*
- *Batch Updates to Improve Performance*
- *Bind to an XmlDataSource Control*
- *Improve XML Manipulation with XPathDocument*
- *Select Within XPathDocument Using XPath*

Your first job is to set up the database connection. You can do this in a number of ways, but it's easiest to click the smart tag and drop down the Choose Data Source list. Click <New data source...>, as shown in Figure 5-1.

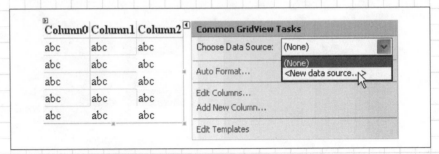

Figure 5-1. Creating a new data source

When you click <New data source...> the Data Source Configuration Wizard opens. For this lab, click Database and then click OK, as shown in Figure 5-2.

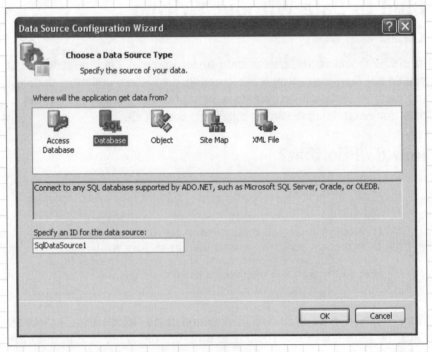

Figure 5-2. The Data Source Configuration Wizard

Chapter 5: Data

The wizard will bring you to the Configure Data Source dialog. Assuming you do not already have a connection to the database with Northwind, click the New Connection... button, as shown in Figure 5-3.

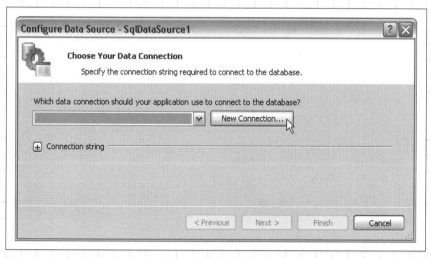

Figure 5-3. Choosing New Connection

This will bring you to the Add Connection step, as shown in Figure 5-4, where you can click the drop down to select the server you want to use, set the password, and then choose the Northwind database. Be sure to click Test Connection to test that you've set it all up properly.

Once the connection is working, click OK and you'll return to the Data Source Configuration Wizard. You should see your connection string in the "Connection string" box (indicating a trusted connection if you used Windows authentication, or your username and password otherwise). Click Next.

Now you are offered the opportunity to store the connection string in your web site's configuration file. This will add a section in *Web.config*, and even better, the configuration will be encrypted. Check the checkbox and name your configuration string.

The next step is to configure your select statement. You can specify columns from a table or view, or you can specify a custom SQL statement or name a stored procedure. For this simple example, drop the Name drop down to Customers and then check the checkbox for every column except ContactTitle.

Notice the buttons for adding a where clause and an order by clause. Click the Advanced Options button, and the Advanced SQL Generation

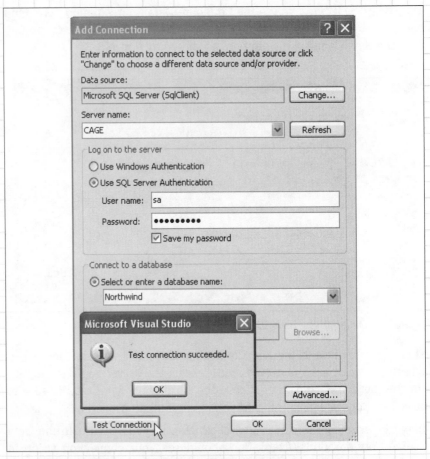

Figure 5-4. Testing the new Northwind connection

Options dialog check the checkbox marked "Generate Insert, Update, and Delete statements." When you do, the "Use optimistic concurrency" option becomes available; check that as well. All of this is shown in Figure 5-5.

The next dialog lets you test your query and see the results so that you can do a sanity check. If you are satisfied, click Finish.

Your GridView is instantly updated and a SqlDataSource control is added to your page. You can modify this data source control at any time by clicking the smart tag and choosing Configure Data Source.

Click the smart tag on the grid. Choose AutoFormat to pick a nice formatting schema. With the smart tag open, check all the checkboxes, turning on features such as paging and sorting that in previous versions you'd have had to write code for, as shown in Figure 5-6.

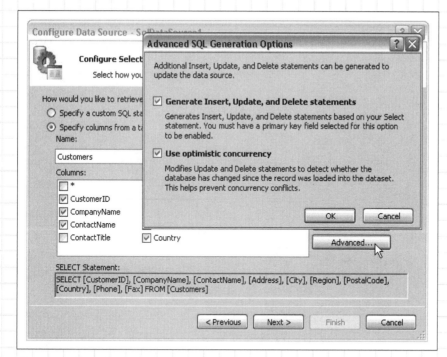

Figure 5-5. The Advanced SQL Generation Options dialog

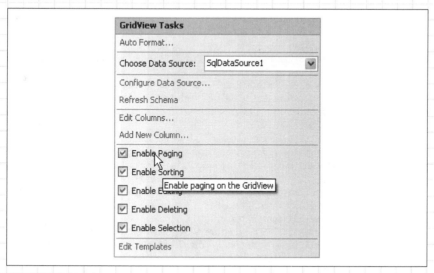

Figure 5-6. Turning on paging, etc.

Click the Source tab and look at the GridView that has been updated for you, as shown in Example 5-1.

Use Windows authentication for a trusted connection.

Optimistic concurrency does not lock records; it adds a where clause to updates and deletes to ensure that the data has not changed since you read it. This is the preferred method for handling concurrency issues.

Example 5-1. Updated GridView

```
<%@ Page Language="C#" AutoEventWireup="true"  CodeFile="Default.aspx.cs"
Inherits="Default_aspx" %>

<!DOCTYPE html PUBLIC "-//W3C//DTD XHTML 1.1//EN" "http://www.w3.org/TR/xhtml11/
DTD/xhtml11.dtd">

<html xmlns="http://www.w3.org/1999/xhtml" >
<head runat="server">
    <title>Untitled Page</title>
</head>
<body>
    <form id="form1" runat="server">
    <div>
        <asp:GridView
        AllowPaging="True"
        AllowSorting="True"
        BackColor="#CCCCCC" BorderColor="#999999"
        BorderStyle="Solid" BorderWidth="3px"
        CellPadding="4"
        CellSpacing="2" DataSourceID="SqlDataSource1"
        ForeColor="Black" ID="GridView1" runat="server">
            <FooterStyle BackColor="#CCCCCC" />
            <Columns>
                <asp:CommandField ShowDeleteButton="True" ShowEditButton="True"
ShowSelectButton="True">
                </asp:CommandField>
            </Columns>
            <RowStyle BackColor="White" />
            <PagerStyle BackColor="#CCCCCC" ForeColor="Black"
HorizontalAlign="Left" />
            <SelectedRowStyle BackColor="#000099" Font-Bold="True"
ForeColor="White" />
            <HeaderStyle BackColor="Black" Font-Bold="True" ForeColor="White" />
            <EditRowStyle Font-Bold="False" Font-Italic="False" />
        </asp:GridView>
        <asp:SqlDataSource
        DeleteCommand="DELETE FROM [Customers] WHERE [CustomerID] = @original_
CustomerID AND [CompanyName] = @original_CompanyName AND [ContactName] =
@original_ContactName AND [ContactTitle] = @original_ContactTitle AND [Address] =
@original_Address AND [City] = @original_City AND [Region] = @original_Region AND
[PostalCode] = @original_PostalCode AND [Country] = @original_Country AND [Phone]
= @original_Phone AND [Fax] = @original_Fax"
        ID="SqlDataSource1" runat="server"
        InsertCommand="INSERT INTO [Customers] ([CustomerID], [CompanyName],
[ContactName], [ContactTitle], [Address], [City], [Region], [PostalCode],
[Country], [Phone], [Fax]) VALUES (@CustomerID, @CompanyName, @ContactName,
@ContactTitle, @Address, @City, @Region, @PostalCode, @Country, @Phone, @Fax)"
        SelectCommand="SELECT [CustomerID], [CompanyName], [ContactName],
[ContactTitle], [Address], [City], [Region], [PostalCode], [Country], [Phone],
[Fax] FROM [Customers]"
```

Example 5-1. Updated GridView (continued)

```
        UpdateCommand="UPDATE [Customers] SET [CompanyName] = @CompanyName,
[ContactName] = @ContactName, [ContactTitle] = @ContactTitle, [Address] =
@Address, [City] = @City, [Region] = @Region, [PostalCode] = @PostalCode,
[Country] = @Country, [Phone] = @Phone, [Fax] = @Fax WHERE [CustomerID] =
@original_CustomerID AND [CompanyName] = @original_CompanyName AND [ContactName]
= @original_ContactName AND [ContactTitle] = @original_ContactTitle AND [Address]
= @original_Address AND [City] = @original_City AND [Region] = @original_Region
AND [PostalCode] = @original_PostalCode AND [Country] = @original_Country AND
[Phone] = @original_Phone AND [Fax] = @original_Fax"
ConflictDetection="CompareAllValues" ConnectionString="<%$ ConnectionStrings:
NorthwindConnectionString %>">
            <DeleteParameters>
                <asp:Parameter Name="original_CustomerID" Type="String" />
                <asp:Parameter Name="original_CompanyName" Type="String" />
                <asp:Parameter Name="original_ContactName" Type="String" />
                <asp:Parameter Name="original_ContactTitle" Type="String" />
                <asp:Parameter Name="original_Address" Type="String" />
                <asp:Parameter Name="original_City" Type="String" />
                <asp:Parameter Name="original_Region" Type="String" />
                <asp:Parameter Name="original_PostalCode" Type="String" />
                <asp:Parameter Name="original_Country" Type="String" />
                <asp:Parameter Name="original_Phone" Type="String" />
                <asp:Parameter Name="original_Fax" Type="String" />
            </DeleteParameters>
            <UpdateParameters>
                <asp:Parameter Name="CompanyName" Type="String" />
                <asp:Parameter Name="ContactName" Type="String" />
                <asp:Parameter Name="ContactTitle" Type="String" />
                <asp:Parameter Name="Address" Type="String" />
                <asp:Parameter Name="City" Type="String" />
                <asp:Parameter Name="Region" Type="String" />
                <asp:Parameter Name="PostalCode" Type="String" />
                <asp:Parameter Name="Country" Type="String" />
                <asp:Parameter Name="Phone" Type="String" />
                <asp:Parameter Name="Fax" Type="String" />
                <asp:Parameter Name="original_CustomerID" Type="String" />
                <asp:Parameter Name="original_CompanyName" Type="String" />
                <asp:Parameter Name="original_ContactName" Type="String" />
                <asp:Parameter Name="original_ContactTitle" Type="String" />
                <asp:Parameter Name="original_Address" Type="String" />
                <asp:Parameter Name="original_City" Type="String" />
                <asp:Parameter Name="original_Region" Type="String" />
                <asp:Parameter Name="original_PostalCode" Type="String" />
                <asp:Parameter Name="original_Country" Type="String" />
                <asp:Parameter Name="original_Phone" Type="String" />
                <asp:Parameter Name="original_Fax" Type="String" />
            </UpdateParameters>
            <InsertParameters>
                <asp:Parameter Name="CustomerID" Type="String" />
                <asp:Parameter Name="CompanyName" Type="String" />
                <asp:Parameter Name="ContactName" Type="String" />
                <asp:Parameter Name="ContactTitle" Type="String" />
                <asp:Parameter Name="Address" Type="String" />
```

Example 5-1. Updated GridView (continued)

```
                <asp:Parameter Name="City" Type="String" />
                <asp:Parameter Name="Region" Type="String" />
                <asp:Parameter Name="PostalCode" Type="String" />
                <asp:Parameter Name="Country" Type="String" />
                <asp:Parameter Name="Phone" Type="String" />
                <asp:Parameter Name="Fax" Type="String" />
            </InsertParameters>
        </asp:SqlDataSource>

    </div>
    </form>
</body>
</html>
```

Before going any further, run the application to see the effect of the changes you've made.

Next, click the smart tag on the DataGrid and click the Edit Columns link to open the Fields dialog, as shown in Figure 5-7.

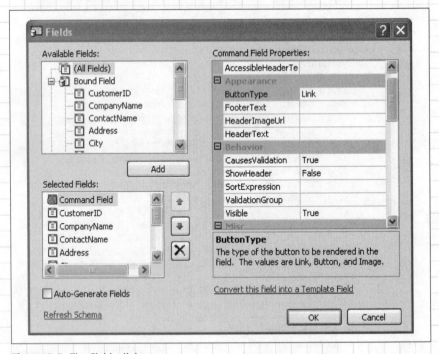

Figure 5-7. The Fields dialog

You have incredible control here. Start in the Command Field Properties window. Notice that ButtonType is set to Link; change it to Button (this changes the update, delete, etc., commands from links to buttons). Scroll down in the Command Field Properties window. You'll see that you can change the text for each button and you can choose to show or hide each command button.

Uncheck the Auto-Generate Fields checkbox. Click each bound field, and click Add to add them to the Selected Fields box (or just double-click the field). As you do, you'll see their properties in the Bound Field Properties window, where you can change the header text (For example, from CompanyName to Company).

When you click OK your changes are reflected in the GridView Designer, as shown in Figure 5-8.

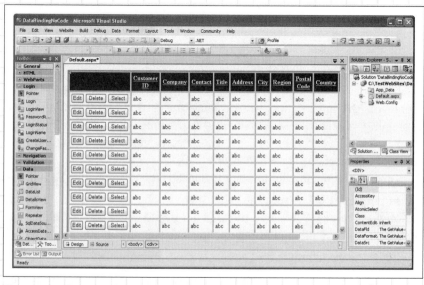

Figure 5-8. Changes reflected in the GridView Designer

What about...

...interacting with the updating GridView? Can I do that even though I created all of this declaratively?

Yes, you can. GridView has a number of events that fire as data is added, updated, etc.

For example, click the GridView control, then click the Events button in the properties window and double-click RowUpdating. This will generate the GridView1_RowUpdating event handler. Try adding this code:

```
void GridView1_RowUpdating(object sender, GridViewUpdateEventArgs e)
{
    string updateCmd = this.SqlDataSource1.UpdateCommand;
}
```

Put a break point on this line of code; run the application, edit the first entry, and change the name to Jesse Liberty.

When you get to the break point press F10 to load the updateCmd string. Drag the string and the GridViewUpdateEventArgs object (e) into the Watch Window.

TIP

You can hover your mouse cursor over an object and a Debugger tool tip will appear with the contents that would be shown in the Watch Window.

The updateCmd string holds the raw SQL statement:

```
"UPDATE [Customers] SET [CompanyName] = @CompanyName, [ContactName] =
@ContactName, [ContactTitle] = @ContactTitle, [Address] = @Address, [City] =
@City, [Region] = @Region, [PostalCode] = @PostalCode, [Country] = @Country,
[Phone] = @Phone, [Fax] = @Fax WHERE [CustomerID] = @original_CustomerID"
```

Where do the substitution values come from? Open e. It contains two interesting collections: NewValues and OldValues. Open NewValues, then open KeyedList and then Values. The second value should be the new value you entered, as shown in Figure 5-9.

Examine the SQL statement. To avoid concurrency issues, the WHERE clause checks to make sure the table has not changed; to do so it needs the original values. You'll find these listed in the OldValues collection, as shown in Figure 5-10.

...what if I want to create these objects programmatically?

No problem. You can instantiate a GridView and/or a DataSourceControl at runtime.

You can create a DataSourceControl using any of its three overloaded constructors (the default constructor, a constructor taking a connection and select strings, or a constructor taking a provider name, a connection string, and a select command string).

You also can create a Parameter object for use with the DataSourceControl, which in turn has four overloaded constructors, allowing you optionally to pass in the name of the parameter, its type, and its default value.

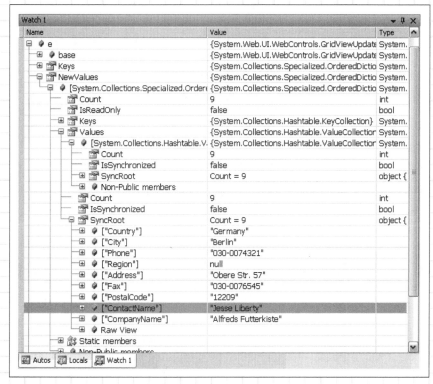

Figure 5-9. New values to update the database

Where can I learn more?

For more on this topic, see my article "ASP.NET 2.0 Data Binding Controls" on the ONDotnet site (*http://www.ondotnet.com*). Also see the article "ASP.NET 2.0 and Data-Bound Controls: A New Perspective" by Dino Esposito in the MSDN Library.

Create Detail Pages

Visual Studio 2005 provides a number of sophisticated, new controls that make it easy for you to interact with data without getting your hands dirty with ADO.NET plumbing. New wizards are available for presenting data in sophisticated ways without writing code.

A classic data requirement is to present the data from a table (for example, the Northwind Orders table) on a form, with text boxes and other controls for interacting with that data. You can do so with virtually no code using the new data-bound controls.

Visual Studio 2005 provides a number of sophisticated new controls that allow you to create flexible datacentric applications without delving into ADO.NET plumbing.

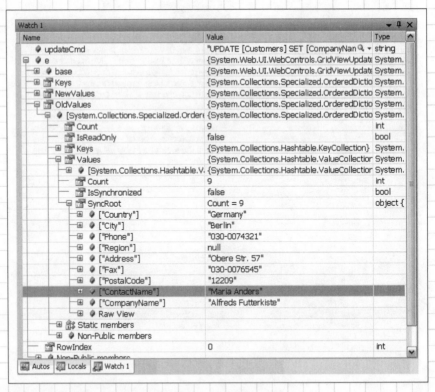

Figure 5-10. Old values to avoid concurrency issues

How do I do that?

To begin, create a new Windows application named OrderDetails. Before adding anything to the form, create a DataSet with a single table based on the Orders table in the Northwind database. To do so, start with the menu choice Data → Show Data Sources.

Click the Add New Data Source link to open the Data Source Configuration Wizard. You can bind your data to a number of different types of data sources, but in this case you want to bind to a database. Click Next, and use the existing connection created in the previous lab (or create a new connection to the Northwind database now).

Click the Orders table in the Data Sources view, and an arrow appears. You can tell the Orders data source that you want to display the data as a DataGridView (as you did in the previous lab) or that you want to display the details. Select Details, as shown in Figure 5-11.

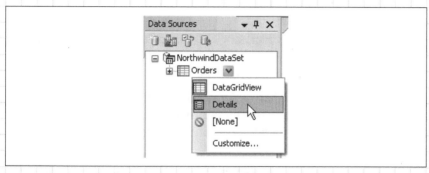

Figure 5-11. Choosing Details in the Orders table

The drop down will close. Drag the Orders table from the Data Sources window onto your form. Labels and data entry controls are created for you, one for each selected field in the Orders table, as shown in Figure 5-12.

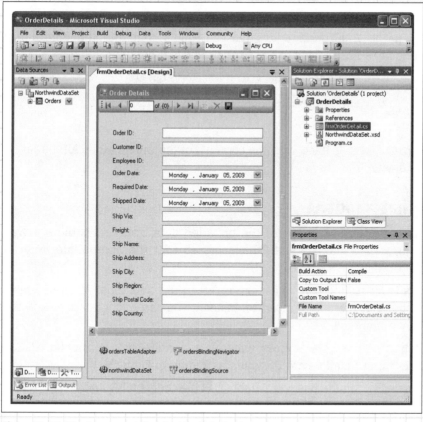

Figure 5-12. The form populated for the Details view

What just happened?

In addition to populating your form, a number of controls are added to your tray, including OrdersTableAdapter, OrdersBindingNavigator, NorthwindDataSet, and OrdersBindingSource.

Table adapters are designer-generated components that connect your DataSet to the underlying data source. Table adapters are similar to data adapters, but they are strongly typed and can contain multiple queries to support multiple tables.

Binding navigators are a standardized, type-safe way to navigate through and manipulate your control. OrdersBindingNavigator is manifested as a toolbar at the top of the form. The BindingSource component simplifies the binding of controls to an underlying data source. It provides an abstraction of the form's data connection, and it passes commands to the underlying data source. BindingNavigator and BindingSource work together as intermediaries between the DataSet and the form's controls.

Open the *frmOrderDetails.cs* file and you'll find that the wizard has added one line of code to the Form_Load event handler:

```
private void Form1_Load(object sender, EventArgs e)
{
    this.ordersTableAdapter.Fill(this.northwindDataSet.Orders);

}
```

TableAdapter is filled with the contents of the Orders table. All the rest is automatic from there.

What about...

...if you don't want to use the provided data controls? Is there a way to pass in a parameter to the query so that the appropriate order is displayed?

Yes there is. You can, of course, revert to the traditional ADO.NET object model, but there is no need to. Instead, you can add a parameter to the query maintained by DataSet.

Return to the Data Sources window and right-click NorthwindDataSet. Select Edit DataSet with Designer, as shown in Figure 5-13.

This will open the Designer. Right-click the Orders table and choose Add → Query, as shown in Figure 5-14.

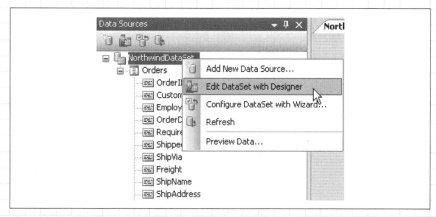

Figure 5-13. Editing the data set

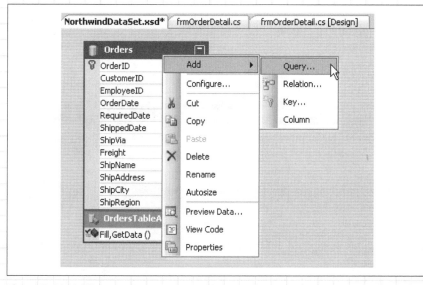

Figure 5-14. Adding a query

This opens the TableAdapter Query Configuration Wizard. Click Next to begin. On the wizard page that opens, choose Use SQL Statements (or if you prefer, create a new stored procedure or use an existing one). The SQL statement we'll create will return one or more rows of data. In the next step in the wizard, modify the query by adding the highlighted text shown in Figure 5-15. Click Next.

In the next wizard step, name your methods for filling and getting the data tables to indicate the parameter you'll use, as shown in Figure 5-16.

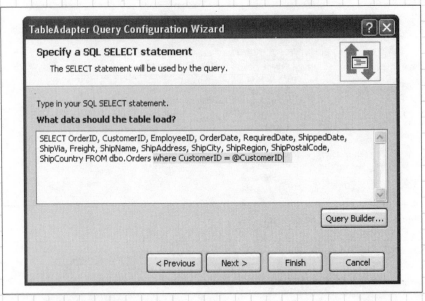

Figure 5-15. Adding the where clause

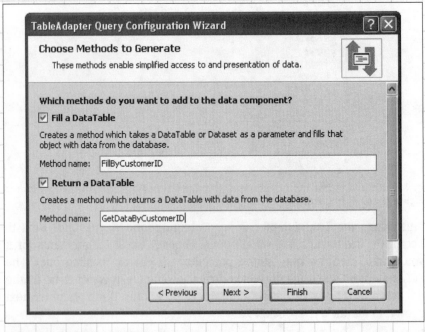

Figure 5-16. Naming the methods

When you click Finish, OrdersTableAdapter has a new method, as shown in Figure 5-17.

Figure 5-17. New table added to OrdersTableAdapter

Alternatively, you can click the smart tag on OrdersTableAdapter (in the tray) and click Add Query, which brings up the Search Criteria Builder that lets you add a new query and name it all in one form, as shown in Figure 5-18.

This second approach automatically adds a tool strip to your form to facilitate searching by the criteria you've set, as shown in Figure 5-19.

Where can I learn more?

MSDN has an excellent overview called "Accessing Data." Pay particular attention to the sections on using the .NET Framework.

Create Master Detail Records

The Orders table is great, but when you look at an order, you want to look at the details of that order as well. The Northwind database establishes a parent-child relationship between each record in the Orders table and one or more orders in the Order Details table. You can reflect that in your application, again with no code.

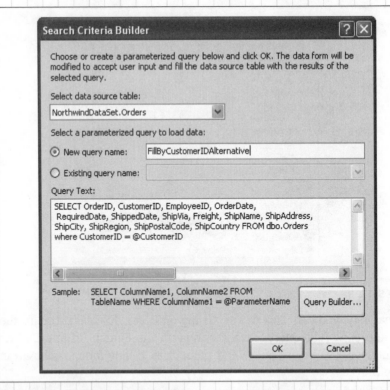

Figure 5-18. The Search Criteria Builder

How do I do that?

Begin by creating a copy of the previous project (using Windows Explorer) and renaming it MasterDetails. Change the name of the solution, the project, and the form.

Open the Data Sources view, right-click NorthwindDataSet, and choose Configure DataSet with Wizard, as shown in Figure 5-20.

Open the Tables in the Data Set, add the Order Details table, and click Finish.

The data set is updated with relation objects based on the appropriate columns; you do not have to write the code to create this relation. Return to the form and reposition half of the controls to the upper half of the form to make room for displaying the order details.

Expand the Orders table. The last node is an OrderDetails node. Drag that onto the form to create a data grid. Hey! Presto! Instant master/detail records!

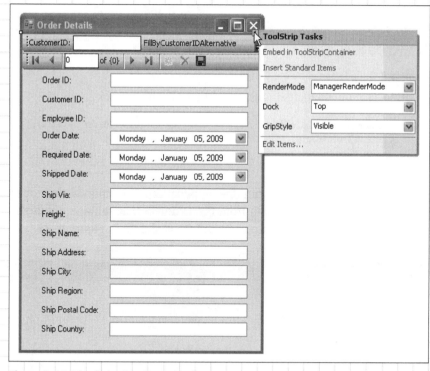

Figure 5-19. The Order Details tool strip

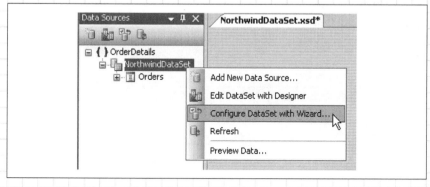

Figure 5-20. Configuring the Northwind data set

What just happened?

Not only was the grid added to your form, but two new controls were added as well: order_DetailsBindingSource and order_detailsTableAdapter.

In addition, code is added to your .cs file to manage filling the two components: one for the order and the other for the order details, as shown in Example 5-2.

Example 5-2. Code added by the Designer

```
private void Form1_Load(object sender, EventArgs e)
{
    this.order_DetailsTableAdapter.Fill(this.northwindDataSet.Order_Details);
    this.ordersTableAdapter.Fill(this.northwindDataSet.Orders);

}
```

Enter the customer ID and run the application. Not only is the order shown, but all the related data from the Order Details table is automatically synchronized to the appropriate order, as shown in Figure 5-21.

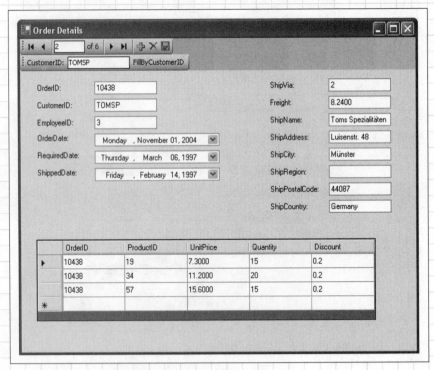

Figure 5-21. Master detail implemented with no code

What about...

...if I want to change the appearance of the details?

You have numerous options. The easiest is to click the smart tag for the grid and then to click Auto Format, as shown in Figure 5-22.

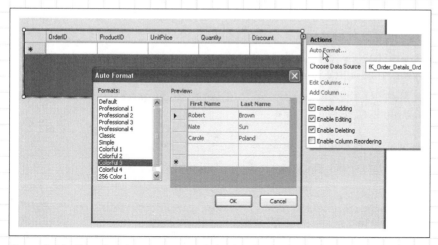

Figure 5-22. Changing the appearance of the details

In addition, you can add or remove columns or change the headers of the columns through the smart tag. You can set other properties through the properties window, and you can respond to dozens of events to interrupt the process and massage either the data or its display in any way you want.

Where can I learn more?

Try the walkthrough "Displaying Related Data on a Windows Form" on the MSDN site.

Get Database Statistics

In tuning your application, it can be very helpful to know how many times you are going to the server, and how much time is being spent doing the work of your application.

If you are using SQL Server, you can use the new RetrieveStatistics method to get diagnostic details.

The RetrieveStatistics method allows you to obtain diagnostic details with a single line of code.

How do I do that?

Create a new C# Windows application (named DataStats). On the form, drag a button and a listbox. Set the button text to Test and set the list-box name to lbStats.

Change the System.Collections.Generic using statement to System. Collections and add a System.Data.SqlClient using statement.

Double-click the button, and in the event handler add the code shown in Example 5-3.

Example 5-3. Measuring SQL statistics

```
private void button1_Click(object sender, EventArgs e)
{
    string connString =
      "Data Source=localhost;Initial Catalog=Northwind;Integrated Security=SSPI";
    SqlConnection conn = new SqlConnection(connString);
    conn.StatisticsEnabled = true;
    conn.Open();
    SqlCommand cmd = new SqlCommand();
    cmd.Connection = conn;

    cmd.CommandText = "Select * from Customers";
    SqlDataReader rdr = cmd.ExecuteReader();
    rdr.Close();
    cmd.CommandText = "Select * from Products";
    rdr = cmd.ExecuteReader();
    rdr.Close();

    for (int i = 0; i < 999; i++)
    {
        cmd.CommandText = "Select * from Customers";
        rdr = cmd.ExecuteReader();
        rdr.Close();
        cmd.CommandText = "Select * from Products";
        rdr.Close();
        rdr = cmd.ExecuteReader();
        rdr.Close();
    }

    conn.Close();

    IDictionary dict = conn.RetrieveStatistics();
    foreach (string key in dict.Keys)
    {
        this.lbStats.Items.Add(key + " = " + dict[key].ToString());
    }
}
```

The results of running this are shown in Figure 5-23.

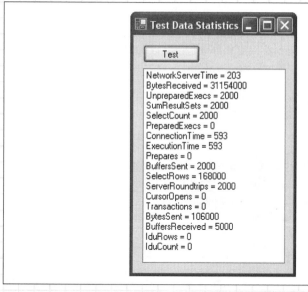

Figure 5-23. SQL statistics

What just happened?

In the button-click handler, you hand-created an SqlConnection object, and you set its StatisticsEnabled property to true. Then you issued two commands, retrieving the results in an SqlDataReader (but you ignored the results).

Next, you repeated this sequence for a total of 1,000 iterations (it's hard to make SQL Server do enough work to register meaningful statistics!).

After you closed the connection you asked the connection for its statistics, which are returned as an IDictionary:

```
IDictionary dict = conn.RetrieveStatistics();
```

You iterated through the dictionary, adding each key and its value to the listbox.

What about...

...resetting the statistics? How do I do that?

Call ResetStatistics on the connection object.

Where can I learn more?

Read through the description of the RetrieveStatistics method in the MSDN Library. For advanced SQL the definitive guide is *The Guru's Guide to Transact SQL* by Ken Henderson (Addison–Wesley).

Batch Updates to Improve Performance

In NET 2.0 you can update the database in batches, reducing the load on your database server.

With .NET 2.0, SqlDataAdapter is upgraded to support the use of batch updates. This can dramatically reduce the number of round trips to the database server, and it can reduce the load on the database, greatly improving overall performance.

How do I do that?

To turn on batch updating, change the UpdateBatchSize property of SqlDataAdapter from the default value of 1 to a higher value. This will allow SqlDataAdapter to group its commands into batches.

To begin, create a new Windows application with controls, as shown in Figure 5-24.

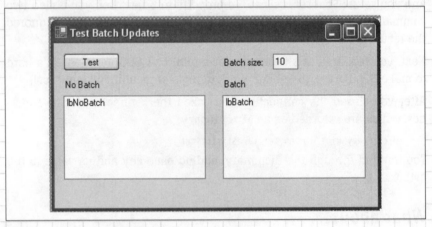

Figure 5-24. The Test Batch Updates dialog

The complete program is shown in Example 5-4.

Example 5-4. Batch-update test code

```
#region Using directives
```

Example 5-4. Batch-update test code (continued)

```csharp
using System;
using System.Collections;
using System.ComponentModel;
using System.Data;
using System.Data.SqlClient;
using System.Drawing;
using System.Windows.Forms;

#endregion

namespace DataStats
{
    partial class Form1 : Form
    {
        public Form1()
        {
            InitializeComponent();
        }

        private void ModifyEachRow(DataSet ds)
        {
            foreach (DataRow row in ds.Tables["Orders"].Rows)
            {
                row["OrderDate"] = DateTime.Now;
            }
        }

        private void ShowStatistics(SqlConnection conn, ListBox lbox)
        {
            IDictionary dict = conn.RetrieveStatistics();
            foreach (string key in dict.Keys)
            {
                lbox.Items.Add(key + " = " + dict[key].ToString());
            }

        }


        private void button1_Click(object sender, EventArgs e)
        {
            string connString = "Data Source=localhost; Initial Catalog=Northwind;";
                connString += "Integrated Security=SSPI";
            SqlConnection conn = new SqlConnection(connString);
            conn.StatisticsEnabled = true;
            conn.Open();
            SqlCommand cmd = new SqlCommand();
            cmd.Connection = conn;

            cmd.CommandText = "Select * from Orders";
            SqlDataAdapter dataAdapter = new SqlDataAdapter(cmd);
            SqlCommandBuilder bldr = new SqlCommandBuilder(dataAdapter);
            DataSet dataset = new DataSet(); ;
```

Example 5-4. Batch-update test code (continued)

```
        dataAdapter.Fill(dataset, "Orders"); // create orders table
        ModifyEachRow(dataset);
        conn.ResetStatistics(); // start statistics clean
        dataAdapter.Update(dataset, "Orders"); // update from the db
        ShowStatistics(conn, this.lbNoBatch);
        dataAdapter.UpdateBatchSize = 10;
        ModifyEachRow(dataset);
        conn.ResetStatistics();
        dataAdapter.Update(dataset, "Orders");
        ShowStatistics(conn, this.lbBatch);

        conn.Close();

    }
  }
}
```

What just happened?

The logic behind this code is to retrieve the complete listing from the *Orders* database into a data set:

```
cmd.CommandText = "Select * from Orders";
SqlDataAdapter dataAdapter = new SqlDataAdapter(cmd);
SqlCommandBuilder bldr = new SqlCommandBuilder(dataAdapter);
DataSet dataset = new DataSet(); ;
dataAdapter.Fill(dataset, "Orders"); // create orders table
```

The SqlCommandBuilder class builds simple update/delete commands for the tables. You will modify each row in the data set by calling ModifyEachRow:

```
private void ModifyEachRow(DataSet ds)
{
    foreach (DataRow row in ds.Tables["Orders"].Rows)
    {
        row["OrderDate"] = DateTime.Now;
    }
}
```

This updates OrderDate to the current time. Now you can reset your statistics and see how long it takes dataAdapter to update the data set:

```
conn.ResetStatistics();
dataAdapter.Update(dataset, "Orders");
ShowStatistics(conn, this.lbNoBatch);
```

You pass the statistics to the first listbox. Then you modify the data again, but this time you set UpdateBatchSize to 10, allowing dataAdapter to update the database with batches:

```
dataAdapter.UpdateBatchSize = 10;
ModifyEachRow(dataset);
```

```
conn.ResetStatistics();
dataAdapter.Update(dataset, "Orders");
ShowStatistics(conn, this.lbBatch);
```

This results in far fewer round trips to the database, as shown in Figure 5-25 (the round-trips statistic has been highlighted).

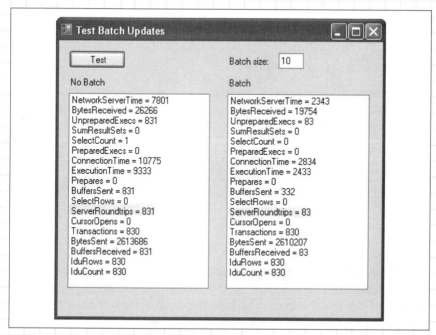

Figure 5-25. Batch updates enabled

Where can I learn more?

To learn more about improving efficiency using batch updates, see the article "ADO.NET 2.0 Feature Matrix" in the MSDN Library.

Bind to an XmlDataSource Control

You can bind to an XML document just as easily as you bind to a database. An XmlDataSource control loads an XML document and exposes its data.

If the XML document you load is hierarchical, the data is exposed hierarchically; which makes it ideal for mapping an XML document to a TreeView control.

You can bind a data control to an XML document using the XmlDataSource control.

How do I do that?

Create a new web application named XMLBinding. Create a new item, an XML file named *BookList.xml*, and add it to the project, as shown in Example 5-5.

Example 5-5. BookList.xml

```xml
<?xml version="1.0" encoding="utf-8" ?>
<Books>
    <book Name="Programming C#">
        <Author Name = "Jesse Liberty" />
        <Publisher PublisherName = "OReilly Media" />
    </book>
    <book Name="Programming ASP.NET">
        <Author Name = "Jesse Liberty" />
        <Author Name = "Dan Hurwitz" />
        <Publisher PublisherName = "OReilly Media" />
    </book>
    <book Name="Visual C# Notebook">
        <Author Name = "Jesse Liberty" />
        <Publisher PublisherName = "OReilly Media" />
    </book>
</Books>
```

Add an XmlDataSource to your *Default.aspx* page. You can do this by dragging one onto your form from the Toolbox, or interestingly, you can drag one from the Toolbox right into the Source view. Add a DataFile attribute and set its value to the name of your *.xml* file:

```
<asp:XmlDataSource ID="XmlDataSource1" Runat="server" DataFile="BookList.
xml" />
```

Now you are ready to add a TreeView control and bind it to this data source. Switch to Design mode and drag the control onto the form. The smart tag allows you to choose the XmlDataSource you just created as the TreeView's data source. Click Auto Format in the smart tag, and choose Windows Help as the format style, as shown in Figure 5-26.

Click Edit TreeNode Databindings... to open the TreeView DataBindings Editor. Set the DataMember for each member in the hierarchy that you want to display (in this case, book, Author, and Publisher), and set the TextField to tell the TreeView which text to use for each DataMember, as shown in Figure 5-27.

The TreeView DataBindings Editor creates HTML that you can see in Source view, as shown in Example 5-6.

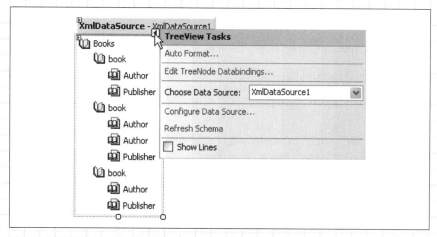

Figure 5-26. Binding the TreeView to XmlDataSource

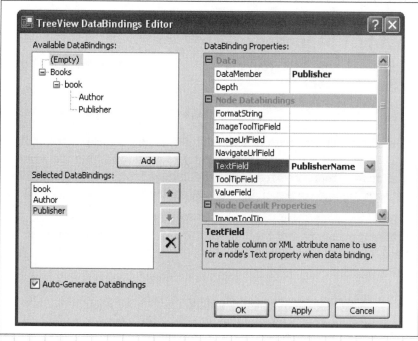

Figure 5-27. The TreeView DataBindings Editor dialog

Example 5-6. Data bindings for TreeView

```
<asp:TreeView ID="TreeView1" Runat="server" DataSourceID="XmlDataSource1"
   ImageSet="WindowsHelp" NodeIndent="15">
   <SelectedNodeStyle BackColor="#B5B5B5" />
   <DataBindings>
       <asp:TreeNodeBinding TextField="Name" DataMember="book" />
```

Example 5-6. Data bindings for TreeView (continued)

```
            <asp:TreeNodeBinding TextField="Name" DataMember="Author" />
            <asp:TreeNodeBinding TextField="PublisherName" DataMember="Publisher" />
        </DataBindings>
        <NodeStyle VerticalPadding="1" Font-Names="Tahoma"
            Font-Size="8pt" HorizontalPadding="5" ForeColor="Black" />
        <HoverNodeStyle Font-Underline="True" ForeColor="#6666AA" />
</asp:TreeView>
```

Note that for each binding, the DataMember corresponds to the DataBinding you added (book, Publisher, Author) and the TextField corresponds to the value you placed in the TextField property, which in turn corresponds to the AttributeName in the XML:

```
        <book Name="Programming ASP.NET">
            <Author Name = "Jesse Liberty" />
            <Author Name = "Dan Hurwitz" />
            <Publisher PublisherName = "OReilly Media" />
        </book>
```

What just happened?

To review, in the XML you created an Author element with a Name attribute:

```
        <Author Name = "Jesse Liberty" />
```

Where possible, I've made the tags self-closing to make the HTML easier to read.

In the TreeView DataBindings Editor you selected Author in the Available DataBindings list and clicked Add, adding it to the Selected DataBindings list. Then you set the TextField property to Name (matching the name of the attribute). Then the TreeView DataBindings Editor emitted HTML into your *.aspx* file that corresponded to these choices:

```
        <asp:TreeNodeBinding TextField="Name" DataMember="Author" />
```

Run the application, and the data in the XML document is bound to the control, as shown in Figure 5-28.

What about...

...if I want a different look and feel for the hierarchy?

Try a different auto format, such as the XP File Explorer format. As shown in Figure 5-29, it is easy to change formats to get the look and behavior you want.

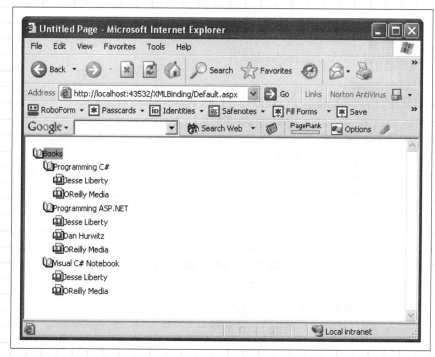

Figure 5-28. XML bound data

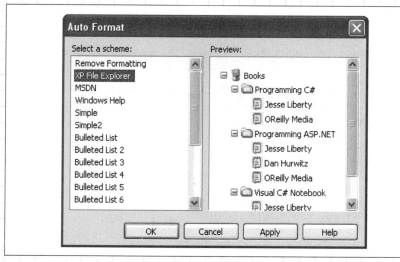

Figure 5-29. Changing the file format

Where can I learn more?

To learn more about the XmlDataSource control, see the article "Data Access in ASP.NET 2.0" in the MSDN Library.

Improve XML Manipulation with XPathDocument

.NET 2.0 provides a new, much-improved XPathDocument class that offers a cursor-based XML reader that is more flexible than XmlWriter and XmlReader and is more efficient (and faster) than XmlDocument.

With XPathDocument it is not necessary for the entire XmlDocument to be loaded into memory. What's more, XPathDocument supports data binding. You can display the XPathDocument in a control just by setting the DataSource property to point to the XPathDocument.

How do I do that?

Create a new Windows program (called XPathDocumentTester). Add an XML document, named *BookList.xml*:

XPathDocument offers a flexible, fast, and efficient mechanism for loading and binding XML documents.

```xml
<?xml version="1.0" encoding="utf-8" ?>
<Books>
    <book>
        <BookName>Programming C#</BookName>
        <Author>Jesse Liberty</Author>
        <Publisher>OReilly Media</Publisher>
    </book>
    <book>
        <BookName>Programming ASP.NET</BookName>
        <Author>Jesse Liberty</Author>
        <Author>Dan Hurwitz</Author>
        <Publisher>OReilly Media</Publisher>
    </book>
    <book>
        <BookName>Visual C# Notebook</BookName>
        <Author>Jesse Liberty</Author>
        <Publisher>OReilly Media</Publisher>
    </book>
    <book>
        <BookName>Visual Basic 2005 Notebook</BookName>
        <Author>Matthew MacDonald</Author>
        <Publisher>OReilly Media</Publisher>
    </book>

</Books>
```

On the form, add a label and a text box, and then add a second label beneath the first one as well, as a button, as shown in Figure 5-30. Name the text box txtBookName, name the second label lblAuthor, and name the button btnFind.

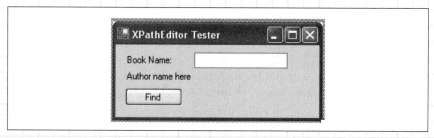

Figure 5-30. The XPathEditor Tester program

The work, of course, is done in the event handler for the Find button, as shown in Example 5-7.

Example 5-7. Using XPathDocument and a navigator

```
#region Using directives

using System;
using System.Collections.Generic;
using System.ComponentModel;
using System.Data;
using System.Drawing;
using System.Windows.Forms;
using System.Xml.XPath;

#endregion

namespace XPathDocumentTester
{
    partial class Form1 : Form
    {
        public Form1( )
        {
            InitializeComponent( );
        }

        private void btnFind_Click(object sender, EventArgs e)
        {
            int numAuthors = 0;
            string authorName = string.Empty;

            // get the file as an XPathDocument
            XPathDocument document = new XPathDocument("..\\..\\BookList.xml");

            // Get a navigator over the document
```

Example 5-7. Using XPathDocument and a navigator (continued)

```
XPathNavigator navigator = document.CreateNavigator( );

navigator.MoveToFirstChild( );    // move to books
navigator.MoveToFirstChild( );    // move to book

do                                // look at each node
{
    // move to entries under book
    navigator.MoveToFirstChild( );

    do                            // look at each sub entry under book
    {
        // if you match the book name, you found the book we want
        if (navigator.Value == txtBookName.Text)
        {
            do                    // moving through the name, author, publisher
            {
                // if you found the author tag, get all the authors
                if (navigator.Name == "Author")
                {
                    if (++numAuthors > 1)    // make a list
                    {
                        authorName += ", ";
                    }
                    authorName += navigator.Value;
                }
            } while (navigator.MoveToNext( ));
        }                         // end if we found the book

    } while (navigator.MoveToNext( ));    // go to the entry under book

    navigator.MoveToParent( );            // done with this book, go up a
level

} while (navigator.MoveToNext( ));        // go to next book

if (numAuthors == 0)
{
    authorName = "Not Found";
}
lblAuthor.Text = authorName;
        }
    }
}
```

What just happened?

The best way to see how this code works is to step through it in the debugger. Place a break point on this line:

```
XPathDocument document = new XPathDocument("..\\..\\BookList.xml");
```

Because the default place to look for the *.xml* file is in the *debug* directory, you are setting the relative path up to where the source code is held.

Run the debugger to this line. Enter the title of a book (e.g., *Programming ASP.NET*) and click Find. The debugger stops at your break point. Press F10 and hover your mouse cursor over the document. You'll find that you have an object of type XPathDocument.

Press F10 to get the navigator. Open the Watch Window and add three entries, as shown in Figure 5-31.

Figure 5-31. Watch Window entries

Your cursor is on this line of code:

```
navigator.MoveToFirstChild( );
```

and navigator.Name is blank. Press F10 and the navigator.Name value changes to Books. You want to go down one more level. Press F10 and the navigator.Name value changes to Book. Aha! Now you are examining a Book node, which is just what you want.

Enter the do loop and execute the MoveToFirstChild command. This sets the navigator.Name value to BookName and the navigator.Value value to Programming C#. This is not the book you are looking for, so the if statement fails, as shown in Figure 5-32.

Press F10 to cycle through the do loop. Finally, you've looked at all the fields for that book and you hit this line:

```
navigator.MoveToParent( );
```

This brings you back up to the *book* level. Continue to press F10 and you move to the next book and then enter the do loop again, where you move to the first child of that book. Now you are ready to examine the book name, and this time you have the right book. The if statement succeeds, so you enter the innermost do loop to iterate through the entries for this book.

When the navigator.Name field is equal to Author you have the right author for the right book, so you can add to the authorName string (the final if statement just puts commas between names for multiple authors).

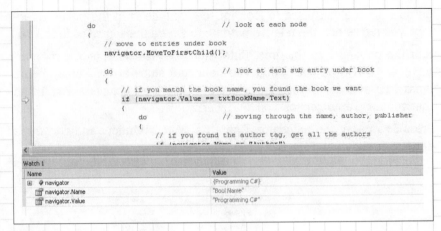

```
        do                              // look at each node
        {
        // move to entries under book
        navigator.MoveToFirstChild();

            do                          // look at each sub entry under book
            {
            // if you match the book name, you found the book we want
            if (navigator.Value == txtBookName.Text)
            {
                do                      // moving through the name, author, publisher
                {
                    // if you found the author tag, get all the authors
                    if (navigator.Name == "Author")
```

Watch 1	
Name	Value
⊞ ◆ navigator	{Programming C#}
📑 navigator.Name	"Bool Name"
📑 navigator.Value	"Programming C#"

Figure 5-32. Not the correct book

When you exit all of this code, you've grabbed the names for the authors of the chosen book and you've displayed them in the label, as shown in Figure 5-33.

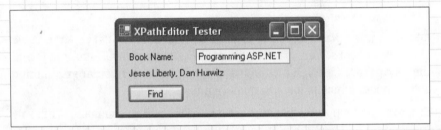

Figure 5-33. Authors retrieved and displayed

What about...

...selecting a portion of the XML document rather than searching the entire document? Can I do that?

Because you know the structure of your document, you can use XPath to narrow the selection. This is shown in the next lab.

Where can I learn more?

Learn more about XPathDocument on the MSDN site in the article titled "XPathDocumentClass." Also, a good weblog article is on DotNetJunkies at *http://dotnetjunkies.com/WebLog/jcmag/archive/2004/02/09/6862.aspx.*

Select Within XPathDocument Using XPath

You can select a portion of the XML document to feed to XPathNavigator to limit the area of your XML document that is parsed or to enhance the efficiency of your application.

To do so, you'll use the SelectNode( ) or SelectNodes( ) methods of the XPathDocument. These methods require an XPath expression to identify which nodes you are looking for.

Simplify your use of XPathNavigator by selecting a portion of the XmlDocument with XPath.

How do I do that?

Make a copy of your previous lab and name it XPathTester. Replace the Find_Click button handler with the code in Example 5-8.

TIP

The simplest way to do this is to copy the directory, rename the new directory, throw away the solution file, open the project, and rename the project. Then edit the code.

Example 5-8. Selecting nodes with XPath

```
private void btnFind_Click(object sender, EventArgs e)
{
    int numAuthors = 0;
    string authorName = string.Empty; ;

    System.Xml.XPath.XPathDocument document =
        new XPathDocument("..\\..\\BookList.xml");
    XPathNavigator navigator = document.CreateNavigator( );

    // selection with filter
    string selectionCriteria = "//Author[../BookName='" + txtBookName.Text +
"']";

    XPathExpression query = navigator.Compile(selectionCriteria);

    // select the matching nodes
    XPathNodeIterator nodes = navigator.Select(query);

    while (nodes.MoveNext( ))
    {
        if (++numAuthors > 1)    // make a list
        {
            authorName += ", ";
        }
```

Example 5-8. Selecting nodes with XPath (continued)

```
        authorName += nodes.Current.Value; // nodeIterator.Current.Value;
    }

    if (numAuthors == 0)
    {
        authorName = "Not Found";
    }
    lblAuthor.Text = authorName;
}
```

TIP

When running, the application looks identical to the previous example.

What just happened?

In this example, instead of looking through all the nodes, you use XPath to find the Author node. You filter that Author node to say that you only want the Author nodes which are within nodes where BookName matches the book name the user entered:

```
string selectionCriteria = "//Author[../BookName='" + txtBookName.Text +
"']";
```

You pass that string to the Compile method of the navigator, which returns an XPathExpression:

```
XPathExpression query = navigator.Compile(selectionCriteria);
```

You feed that XPathExpression to the Select method of the XPathNavigator which returns an XPathNodeIterator that you can use to iterate over the matching nodes:

```
XPathNodeIterator nodes = navigator.Select(query);
```

What about...

...retrieving the data values as strongly typed values? Can I do that?

Yes, you can do that. Instead of using the string value returned by the Value property, you can use one of the strongly typed properties.

These include:

- ValueAsBoolean
- ValueAsDateTime
- ValueAsDecimal

- ValueAsDouble
- ValueAsInt32
- ValueAsInt64
- ValueAsList
- ValueAsSingle

Where can I learn more?

XPath is a big topic, and tutorials are available that are dedicated to teaching how to use XPath well. One good starting point is *http://www.w3schools.com/*. Another tutorial is available at *http://java.sun.com/webservices/docs/1.3/tutorial/doc/JAXPXSLT3.html*.

Index

We'd like to hear your suggestions for improving our indexes. Send email to *index@oreilly.com*.

M

MacNeil, Robert, 33
ManageRoles.aspx, 128–132
mask values, 83
masked editing control, 80–87
MaskedTextBox
  BeepOnError property, 82
  Mask property, 82
  PromptChar property, 82
MaskedTextBox class
  learning more about, 84
MaskedTextBox control, 80–84
  learning more about, 84
  MaskCompleted property, 82
  Text property, 82
masks, creating your own, 83
master detail records, 189–193
master pages, 164–171
  adding content pages that
    use, 167–169
  asp:contentPlaceHolder
    control, 164–169
  designing, 164–166
  in Display view, 166
  learning more about, 171
  modifying on the fly, 170
  nesting, 169–170
  QuickStart tutorial, 171
McConnell, Steve, 69
membership, learning more
    about, 137
MenuStrip control, 79
methods, anonymous (see anonymous
    methods)
methods and generics, 11
multithreaded applications, 93–99
  BackgroundWorker object (see
    BackgroundWorker object)

N

namespace keyword, 40
.NET 2.0
  binding to data without writing
    code (see data binding)
  MaskedTextBox control (see
    MaskedTextBox control)
  SqlDataAdapter and batch
    updates, 196–199
    test code, 196–198
    UpdateBatchSize property, 196

support for safe asynchronous
    tasks, 93–99
SystemSounds class (see
    SystemSounds class)
ToolStrip control (see tool strips)
WebBrowser control (see
    WebBrowser control)
XPathDocument class (see
    XPathDocument class)
New Connection... button, 175
<New data source...> command, 174
new keyword, 4
New Web Site dialog box, 110, 111
Northwind, 173
NorthwindDataSet control, 186
Noyes, Brian, 107
nullable Boolean operators, 39
nullable types, 35–39
  learning more about, 39

O

online resources, xiv
order_DetailsBindingSource
    control, 191
order_detailsTableAdapter
    control, 191
OrdersBindingNavigator control, 186
OrdersBindingSource control, 186
OrdersTableAdapter control, 186
O'Reilly's ONDotnet.com, 73
Osherove, Roy, 99
overloaded constructors, 182

P

Parameter object, 182
partial classes
  warnings, 32
partial keyword, 31–33
partial modifier, 32
partial type definitions, 32
partial types, learning more about, 33
PasswordRecovery control, 123–125
passwords, if users forget, 123
persistence that goes beyond session
    state, 140
personalization, 140
  learning more about, 146, 151, 155
personalized web sites, 137–146
  Add Profile Info hyperlink, 143
  adding data to user's profile, 140

About the Author

Jesse Liberty is the author of such O'Reilly titles as *Programming C#*, *Programming ASP.NET*, and *Learning C#*, and a dozen other books on web and object-oriented programming. Jesse is the president of Liberty Associates, Inc. (*http://www.LibertyAssociates.com*), where he provides .NET training, contract programming, and consulting. He is a former vice president of electronic delivery for Citibank, and a former distinguished software engineer and architect for AT&T, Ziff Davis, Xerox, and PBS.

Colophon

Our look is the result of reader comments, our own experimentation, and feedback from distribution channels. Distinctive covers complement our distinctive approach to technical topics, breathing personality and life into potentially dry subjects.

The *Developer's Notebook* series is modeled on the tradition of laboratory notebooks. Laboratory notebooks are an invaluable tool for researchers and their successors.

Sarah Sherman was the production editor, and Audrey Doyle was the copyeditor for *Visual C# 2005: A Developer's Notebook*. Katherine T. Pinard was the proofreader. Jamie Peppard and Claire Cloutier provided quality control. Lydia Onofrei provided production assistance. Julie Hawks wrote the index.

Edie Freedman designed the cover of this book. Karen Montgomery produced the cover layout with Adobe InDesign CS using the Officina Sans and JuniorHandwriting fonts.

David Futato designed the interior layout. This book was converted by Joe Wizda to FrameMaker 5.5.6 with a format conversion tool created by Erik Ray, Jason McIntosh, Neil Walls, and Mike Sierra that uses Perl and XML technologies. The text font is Adobe Boton; the heading font is ITC Officina Sans; the code font is LucasFont's TheSans Mono Condensed, and the handwriting font is a modified version of JuniorHandwriting made by Tepid Monkey Foundry, and modified by O'Reilly. The illustrations that appear in the book were produced by Robert Romano, Jessamyn Read, and Lesley Borash using Macromedia FreeHand MX and Adobe Photoshop 6. This colophon was written by Colleen Gorman.

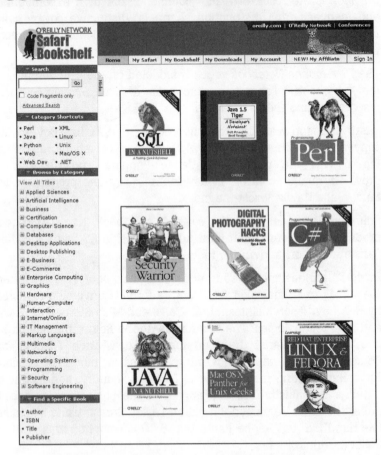